CW00925766

WALKING IN THE
SOUTH WALES VALLEYS

Walking in the South Wales Valleys

Hill and Heritage trails in Glamorgan and Gwent

Aled Elwyn Jones

First published in 2016

ISBN: 978-1-84524-240-4

Cover design: Eleri Owen

Published by Gwasg Carreg Gwalch
Llanrwst
Wales

www.carreg-gwalch.com

I Mam a Dad

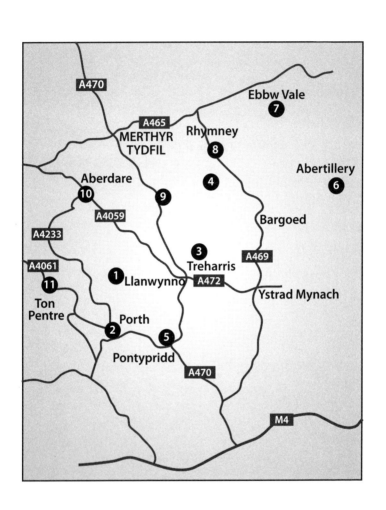

A470

Ebbw Vale
7

A465

MERTHYR
TYDFIL

Rhymney
8

Abertillery
6

4

Aberdare
10

9

A4059

Bargoed

A4233

3

A469

A4061

Treharris

1 Llanwynno

A472

11

Ystrad Mynach

Ton
Pentre

Porth

2

5

Pontypridd

A470

M4

Contents

Introduction

Landscape

To refer to the area covered by this book as 'The Valleys' is to tell only half the story of its landscape. A more rounded picture is given when we remember that this part of south Wales was commonly known in pre-industrial times as *Y Blaenau* – a name which might be best translated as 'The Upland Frontiers', and which distinguished these parts of Glamorgan (*Morgannwg*) and Gwent from the more low-lying *Y Fro* (The Vale) along the Severn Estuary. Together, the valleys and the *blaenau* make for a varied and interesting landscape for the walker to explore.

Though there are other valleys in south Wales, most notably the Usk (*Wysg*) and Wye (*Gwy*), the 'south Wales valleys' as a collective are those that lie within the south Wales coalfield, stretching from the Gwendraeth in the west to the Llwyd in the east. There are around twenty significant valleys and rivers, plus numerous more side-valleys and tributaries. These valleys have been shaped over the millennia not only by their rivers, but also on more than one occasion by ice age glaciers. It is the latter which are responsible for the distinctive U-shaped, steep-sided profile of many valleys, and the glacial cwms, or corries, sometimes found at their heads.

Together these valleys and their rivers dissect and drain an upland plateau, which is the southernmost part of the highland massif that makes up the entire spine of Wales. Large tracts of this moorland plateau are over 400 meters above sea level, reaching 580 meters on Mynydd Coety in the east of the coalfield and 600 meters at Craig y Llyn in the north west. There are several hilltops that are higher than any point in Exmoor or the North York Moors – two of Britain's highland National Parks.

The area is split in two by the long, deep, and straight Neath (*Nedd*) valley which, unlike most others, follows the line of a major geological fault. The Neath and the other rivers to its west flow in a generally south-westerly direction, while to its east the predominant flow is south-easterly. At the same time, the plateau to its west is lower than to the east. The Neath therefore forms a convenient boundary for this volume of walks, which concentrates on the valleys and hills to its east.

Geology
Both the area's physical geography and human history have been shaped by its geology. The south Wales coalfield is in geological terms a large basin, or syncline, comprising a succession of carboniferous (359 – 299 million years old) rock layers that all rise towards the edges and dip towards the centre of the area. At the rim of the basin – along the heads of the valleys in the north, and along the low ridges that border the Vale in the south – are found an outer ring of limestone outcrops, and an inner ring of coal measures. The coal measures themselves include iron ore as well as seams of coal amongst layers of shale and sandstone, and it was this easy accessibility of ore, limestone and coal that made Merthyr Tydfil, Ebbw Vale and Blaenavon perfect locations for ironworks from the 18th century onwards. The presence of coal at the surface in this area has also made open-cast mining possible: an activity that continues along the heads of the valleys today.

Towards the interior of the basin, the coal measures are either restricted to the bases of the hills and the valley floors or, more commonly, are completely buried below the surface. The coal here was therefore more difficult to extract, a situation exacerbated by the fact that the most productive and high-quality seams are found towards the bottom of the measures. Deep pits were therefore needed to reach the best coal in the valleys interior, with mines at such places such as Treharris, Abercynon and Nantgarw working seams over 700 meters below the surface.

Above the coal measures lies a succession of Pennant sandstones: the hard, solid rocks that make up the hills of the *Blaenau*. This stone is very suitable for building, and so the steep valley slopes are dotted with old quarries where it was extracted to build the towns and villages below. The Pennant measures also include some lower-quality seams of coal, which could be mined by digging levels into the hillside. Many of the hillside paths in this book follow the lines of the tracks and tramways that serviced these quarries and levels.

The changing landscape

The valleys today are unrecognisable from how they were only a generation ago. Gone for the most part are the once ubiquitous black spoil heaps. The majority have been removed or landscaped, and those that remain have been greened by a cover of vegetation. Fish are found again in once sterile rivers. The reclamation of some sites by nature is impressive indeed: places such as Parc Taf Bargoed and Parc Cwm Darran, with their fishing lakes and nature reserves, were once vast industrial sites where wildlife stood little chance, and where no-one would have thought to go for a walk.

This recent transformation may be significant, but it is nowhere near as spectacular as the metamorphosis undergone when these valleys were industrialised in the first place. Despite the 'greening' of the last few decades, it is still difficult to visualise what these valleys were like until only two hundred years ago. Some idea can be had though from the testimony of early travellers such as B. H. Malkin, who toured south Wales in 1803, and who was struck by the wildness and natural beauty he found in the valleys. Travelling up the Rhondda Fawr, he remarks that '[t]*he upper part of Ystradyvodwg parish is as untameably wild as any thing that can be conceived; and the few, who have taken the pains to explore the scattered magnificence of South Wales agree in recommending this untried route to the English traveller, as one of the most curious and striking in the principality, not excepting the more known and frequented tour of the northern counties.*'

Even in Malkin's day however, industry had began to make its presence felt. The modern-day walker will often be struck by the suddeness of the transition from town to country, or from post-industrial landscape to untouched moorland, and vice-versa. Malkin describes just this sensation on travelling up the Cynon valley towards Aberdare: '*It is a bold and rich scene, and the meadows form a most pleasing fore-ground.... It produces a sudden and rather inexplicable sensation in the mind, to meet with the modern improvements of scientific ingenuity, and the activity of commercial enterprise, in a country which seems to have precluded all such possibilities, and appeared but just before like the very head-quarters of solitude.*'

It is that ever-present contrast between human activity and nature, living cheek-by-jowl with each other in the most confined of spaces, which still makes the valleys such a unique landscape to explore today.

History

The history of the valleys over the last two hundred years has in many ways been the driving force of the development of modern Wales. Previously as isolated and pastoral as any other upland part of the country, the valleys were utterly transformed by the industrial revolution of the 18th and 19th centuries. Such was the impact of their sudden development that they, in turn, changed Wales. In the century from the founding of the Dowlais Ironworks in 1759, the valleys went from inaccessible rural backwaters to being the most important centre of iron and coal production in the world. The towns that grew around the new industries – Merthyr Tydfil being the earliest and most important example – gave Wales its first ever major urban settlements. The drive to take the heavy produce to its markets led to the development of a transportation network; first canals, and then railways and roads, and gave birth to the major ports at Swansea, Cardiff, Newport that eventually outgrew the valley towns they were built to serve.

There was a demographic transformation too. The demand for manpower for first the iron and then the coal industries led to explosive levels of inward migration and population growth. In the most spectacular example, the population of the Rhondda grew from fewer than 1,000 in 1851 to over 150,000 in 1911. Initially, the migrants came mostly from other parts of Wales. As a result, Welsh – uniquely among the native languages of Britain and Ireland – became the language of an urban working class, leading to a 19th century cultural renaissance that had towns such as Pontypridd and Aberdare at its centre. When the supply of labour from rural Wales could no longer fulfil the demand however, immigrants came increasingly from other parts of Britain, Ireland, and beyond, leading to the spread of English from the mid 1800s onwards. Despite the westward advance of English, the Glamorgan valleys remained majority Welsh-speaking at the turn of the 20th century, and places such as Treorchy and Aberdare were still so until the Second World War. Some communities in the western valleys still are today. Today, the language is undergoing a renaissance in the central and eastern valleys, which have been at the vanguard of Welsh medium education since the establishment of Ysgol Rhydfelen near Pontypridd in 1962.

The valleys were also an early hotbed of political radicalism, and have played a key part in the history of the left in Welsh and

British politics. During the Merthyr Uprising of 1831, workers marched under a red flag for the first time, whilst the Chartist Newport Rising of 1839 is considered the last large-scale armed rebellion to take place in mainland Britain. In 1900, Keir Hardie became the first ever Labour Party MP when he was elected in Merthyr Tydfil and Aberdare, while Ebbw Vale MP Aneurin Bevan took inspiration from the Tredegar Medical Aid Society to establish the NHS in the 1940s. The valleys have also played an important part in the development of Welsh nationhood in the second half of the 20th century; Plaid Cymru has made occasional breakthroughs in places including Rhondda, Merthyr and Caerphilly since the 1960s, and the size of the Yes vote throughout the area was crucial in securing devolution in the 1997 referendum.

The south Wales coal industry reached its zenith at the end of the First World War when 232,000 men worked in a total of 620 mines across the coalfield. A process of decline set in thereafter, accelerated by the depression in the 1930s, and given only a short reprieve by the rise in demand during World War Two, to conclude with the closing of the last deep mines in the 1990s. Even after a century of population loss – Merthyr Tydfil's population has dropped by a quarter since 1921, while the Rhondda's has more than halved – the valleys are still home to over a quarter of the Welsh population. The mines and furnaces may be long gone, except for those preserved as tourist attractions and museums, but much of the built heritage remains. The iconic rows of terraced houses still cling precariously to the steep hillsides, and there have survived too some fine examples of the two pillars of valleys society – the nonconformist chapels and the working men's institutes, though many more have been sadly lost. The walks in this book take in examples of them all, and much more, including tramways, tips and canals.

Given the exceptional story of the last two hundred years, it would be easy to overlook the thousands of years of human history that preceded them. Unsurprisingly, older historic monuments have survived best on the relatively undisturbed hills, and the sites visited on the walks provide an insight into the human history of the area stretching from the Bronze Age to the dawn of the industrial area. Together they cover a period of 4,000 years during which the hills and valleys came under the influence of a succession of peoples and cultures.

The very oldest evidence of human activity in south Wales has been found along the coast, but the uplands too appear to have been continuously inhabited since the dawn of civilisation. A carved wooden post found during the construction of a windfarm above the Rhondda Fach, and thought to mark an ancient boundary or sacred site, has been dated to 6,250 years ago; just around the period when Stone Age humans in Britain were transitioning from a nomadic, hunter-gatherer existence to more settled societies based on agriculture. Several Bronze Age burial sites and cairns have also survived, and a 20th century find of bronze and iron objects at Llyn Fawr at the head of the Cynon Valley was so significant that the 'Llyn Fawr Phase' is the name given by archaeologists to the final period of the Bronze Age in Britain, between 800 and 700BC.

By the Iron Age, we know not only that the area's inhabitants had developed complex enough societies to construct hill forts at places such as Maendy Camp, Rhiwsaeson and Twmbarlwm, but also – thanks to the Romans – we have the first evidence of their appearance and character, as well as a name to call them by. The Silures were a Brythonic tribe or association of tribes, that inhabited all of south Wales east of the Loughor (a boundary between south and west Wales that it still recognised today) including modern Glamorgan, Gwent and Brecknockshire. The

Roman historian Tacitus described their swarthy features and dark, curly hair. He also commented on the Silures' fierce resistance to the Roman invaders, observing that 'neither cruelty nor clemency would change them'. It took over 30 years of military campaigns before the Silures were finally subdued, and the Romans left their mark on the area with forts at Gelligaer, Caerphilly, Penydarren and Neath, and marching camps such as that at Twyn-y-Briddallt.

Following a period of increasing instability, the Romans left Britain at the turn of the 5th century, and in post-Roman times, the area was initially divided between a number of small kingdoms, whose cultures combined Silurian and Roman influences, but who increasingly came to see themselves as *Cymry* (Welsh) as the Anglo-Saxons established their control over England to the east. Though borders were never stable, power in south Wales eventually coalesced around the Kingdoms of Glamorgan and Gwent, while the Kindgom of Brycheiniog represented another centre of power and influence to the north.

The Welsh kings had to battle a succession of invaders, including Viking, Irish and Saxon, but it was the Normans who were to have a lasting impact. Following the conquest of England in 1066, the coastal lowlands of Gwent and Glamorgan were immediately vulnerable to Norman incursions, and the Earl of Gloucester succeeded in deposing the last King of Glamorgan, Iestyn ap Gwrgant, in around 1090. But while the plains were lost, upland Glamorgan and Gwent remained in Welsh hands for some time, and provided a base for Welsh attacks and uprisings against the new overlords. Most famously, Ifor Bach, Lord of Senghenydd, raided Cardiff Castle in 1158 and managed to kidnap the Earl, his wife, and son, and held them to ransom for the return of his lands. Ifor's descendant Llywelyn Bren led a more widespread revolt against the Normans in 1316.

The Norman Marcher Lords consolidated their hold and established castles at Caerphilly, Llantrisant and elsewhere, though they were fewer in number in the *Blaenau* compared to the coastal areas of Glamorgan and Gwent. They also built new churches, often at sites that had been consecrated for centuries by Celtic saints, and the Cistercians with their abbeys at Llantarnam and Neath became major landowners in the area.

Many of the Norman castles were attacked and seized during the revolt of Owain Glyndŵr in 1400-04, but after the Acts of Union of 1536 and 1542, Wales became fully politically and legally – though not culturally or lingustically – integrated with England. The Marcher Lordships that had been the personal fiefdoms of powerful noblemen were abolished, and the area administered by the counties of Glamorgan and Monmouthshire: administrative units that survived into the 20th century.

The Walks

The eleven walks in this book cover the central and eastern parts of the valleys area, from Maesteg in the Llynfi valley in the west to Blaenavon on the Lwyd river in the east. Each walk combines industrial landscapes and unspoilt countryside, finding places of historical interest in both.

The categorisations of easy, medium and difficult below are inevitably subjective, and are intended only as a guide to how the walks compare to the others in the book, rather than how they might relate to some universal standard: some will find all the walks to be easy, whilst others will find even the easier ones a challenge.

Circular Walks

1. **Llanwynno and Cwm Clydach**: 11 miles, Easy. Exploring the hilly countryside between the Cynon and Rhondda Fach, including a historic church and secluded waterfall. Some riverside and woodland walking – good paths throughout.

2. **Porth, Penrhys and the Rhondda Fach**: 10.5 miles, Moderate. Taking in the ridges either side of the Rhondda Fach, including the historic shrine of Penrhys and the landmark Tylorstown Tip, with impressive views. Mixture of paths and open country with two steep climbs.

3. **Mynydd Cilfach yr Encil from Parc Taf Bargoed**: 11.5 miles, Difficult. An at times steep hill-walk high above the Taf and Taf Bargoed valleys and Merthyr Tydfil, starting and ending at Parc Taf Bargoed.

4. **Gelligaer Common and Cefn Brithdir**: 11 miles, Moderate. Mostly upland walking along historic Gelligaer Common and Cefn Brithdir, including 5th century Capel Gwladys and Parc Cwm Darran.

5. **Mynydd Eglwysilan, Pontypridd and Senghenydd**: 11 miles, Easy/Moderate. Varied walk full of historical interest in and around Pontypridd and Senghenydd, and open moorland on Mynydd Eglwysilan.

6. **Abertillery and Blaenavon**: 14.5 miles, Difficult. A long walk that can be adapted into two shorter ones. Taking in the UNESCO World Heritage Sites of Blaenavon, and open moorland of Mynydd James and Coety Mountain.

Linear Walks

The five linear walks together make up a continuous 53 mile long route, traversing a total of thirteen valleys and the intervening ridges, from Ebbw Vale in the east to Maesteg in the west. The walks take advantage of the valleys' railway network, with each one starting and ending at a train station.

7. **Ebbw Vale to Pontlottyn**: 10 miles, Easy/Moderate. Taking in the Ebbw, Sirhywi and Rhymney valleys, and Cefn Manmoel and Mynydd Bedwellty ridges, including a hillside cholera cemetery at Cefn Goleu, Tredegar.

8. **Pontlottyn to Troedyrhiw**: 8 miles, Easy/Moderate. From the Rhymney valley to the Taff via the Taff Bargoed. A variety of landscapes, including Carn y Bugail with its Stone Age and Roman sites, Bedlinog village, and Mynydd Cilfach-yr-Encil high above Merthyr Tydfil.

9. **Troedyrhiw to Aberdare**: 11 miles, Moderate. The Taff and Cynon valleys. The first section is flat as it follows the Taff along old tramways and towpaths, including through Aberfan. The second part a ridge-walk along Twyn Brynbychan and Mynydd Merthyr before descending to Aberdare.

10. **Aberdare to Ton Pentre**: 11 miles, Moderate/Difficult. From the Cynon to the Rhondda Fawr, via the Aman and Rhondda Fach valleys. Including historic Aberdare and Ferndale, and a Roman camp at Twyn y Briddallt.

11. **Ton Pentre to Maesteg**: 13 miles, Difficult. From the Rhondda Fawr to the Llynfi, via the Ogmore and Garw. The most mountainous scenery of all the walks, including glacial cwms and steep escarpments, with climbs to match. Including pre-historic sites at Maendy Camp and Crug yr Afan.

Rights of Way and Access Land

The walks in this book make use of Rights of Way including public footpaths, bridleways and byways, and of Access Land designated under the Countryside and Rights of Way Act 2000. All of these are clearly shown on the Ordnance Survey Explorer map recommended for each walk.

At the time of writing, the only potential obstacles found on any of the routes were some patches of bracken (in summer) and the odd padlocked gate. Gates are often secured to prevent illegal access by off-road vehicles, and where they are on a Right of wWy or access land the walker has every right to climb over them in the same way as they would a stile, though you should be careful not to cause any damage.

Maintenance of Rights of Way is the responsibility of local authorities, who also work with landowners to ensure that open access land is accessible. The walks in this book cover Bridgend, Rhondda Cynon Taf, Merthyr Tydfil, Blaenau Gwent, Caerphilly and Torfaen local authorities. You can help the walkers who come after you by reporting any obstructions or other problems to the relevant authority. Any instances of fly-tipping – a sadly all-too-common problem – should be reported to the same authorities. You should observe the Countryside Code at all times, including leaving gates as you find them, keeping dogs under control, and taking your litter home.

Acknowledgements

I am indebted to many people for their assistance in putting together this book. Rights of Way and Definitive Map officers at several local authorities provided helpful advice and information, in particular Andrew Flemming (Blaenau Gwent), Jamie Gulliford (Merthyr Tydfil), Stefan Denbury (Caerphilly), and Ceri Davies (Rhondda Cynon Taf), and I am grateful to Ifor Coggan of Fochriw History for his assistance with some historical details for Walk 4.

Dafydd Evans, Gwion Evans, Hefin Rees and Katy McGavin provided welcome company as I researched the walks, and I am particularly grateful to Tony Thomas, Richard Bellinger, Tim Roberts and Sara Bines for giving of their time to check the routes, and advise on where the draft instructions were inaccurate or unclear. Thanks too to Betsan for her patience and support throughout.

Llanwynno and Cwm Clydach

1. Llanwynno and Cwm Clydach

Approx distance: *11 miles / 17.5 km*
Approx time: *5.5 hours*
O.S Maps: *1: 50,000 OS Landranger Sheet 170*
1: 25,000 OS Explorer Sheet 166 (recommended)
Start: *The walk starts and ends opposite the church in Llanwynno, Grid Ref. ST 030 956. The post code for the start point is CF37 3PH.*
Access: *Llanwynno stands on the hill between the Cynon and Rhondda valleys at the intersection of three un-named minor roads. You can access these roads from either Ynysybwl, Pontypridd, Perthcelyn (Cynon valley) or Ferndale (Rhondda Fach). Use the sat nav if you have one!*
Parking: *Free car park in Llanwynno, opposite church.*
Terrain: *Mostly along forestry tracks and clear paths, with some short sections across farmland and along minor roads. There is a total ascent of around 350 meters / 1,155 feet.*
Please note: *Some sections can be muddy. The route follows footpaths that pass through a farmyard and the garden of a cottage. Resident dogs may be present at both locations, and there will be sheep and cattle on the farmland sections, so please keep your own dogs on a lead.*
Facilities: *Brynffynnon Hotel at start point in Llanwynno serves food and real ales (closed Monday). If neccessary, a short diversion will take you to facilities in Ynysybwl village.*

Points of Interest

1. Llanwynno Church

The discovery during a 19th century restoration of a fragment of a cross dating back to around the 9th century suggests that a place of worship has existed here since pre-Norman times. Much of the church we see today, however, dates back to that 1893 restoration, except for the walls of the nave, chancel and porch and the chancel itself, which are medieval in origin, possibly dating back to the early 13th century.

The holy well of St Gwynno is located just to the east of the churchyard, and has been a place of pilgrimage since medieval times. It is believed that Saint Gwynno himself lived here during

Guto Nyth Brân

the 6th century. As well as giving his name to this church and parish, he is also, along with Illtyd and Tyfodwg, thought to be one of the three founding saints commemorated in the name of Llantrisant.

In the churchyard is the grave and memorial stone of Guto Nyth Brân (Griffith Morgan, 1700–1737). Legend has it that Guto was the fastest runner of his age (indeed, of any age!). He was so fast that he could run the 7 miles from his home near Porth to Pontypridd and back before the kettle had boiled, or blow out a candle and be in bed

Pistyll Goleu Waterfall

before the light went out. After a long career beating all comers and earning a small fortune in prize money, he died at the age of 37 after his last race, when he ran the 12 miles from Newport to Bedwas in 53 minutes.

2. Pistyll Goleu Waterfall
Hidden away in the depths of Llanwynno Forest, the unsuspecting walker could easily pass right by this wonderfully secluded waterfall without ever knowing it was there. Wooden steps lead from the forestry track to the bottom of the waterfall. The redish colour of the water shows the presence of iron in the underlying rocks.

3. Lady Windsor Colliery
Operational from 1884 to 1988, at its peak the colliery employed over a thousand people. The opening of the colliery transformed

Ynysybwl almost overnight: the 300 workers' cottages built in 1886 totally transformed the small rural village which only five years earlier had had a total population of only 270. New road and rail connections would soon follow. Owned by David Davies' Ocean Steam Company, the mine produced some of the highest quality steam coal available, with customers including the Admiralty and the prestigious Cunard Line.

4. Capel y Fanhalog and Capel Bethel

What is now known as Bethel Cottage was once Capel Fanhalog: one of the earliest Calvinistic Methodist chapels built in what was at the time still an agricultural area. In the early days worshipers came from as far afield as Abercynon and the lower Rhondda. Established in 1786, it was abandoned as a place of worship in 1876 when the new, larger, Capel Bethel was built between it and the road below. Bethel itself closed in 1977, and followed its predecessor in being converted into a private dwelling – Bethel House. The house that stands between them, Glandwr, is the old manse. Built in 1914, it replaced an older building which had provided lodgings for visiting travellers and preachers. While Bethel House is stll very much recognisable as a chapel building from the outside, the same is not true of the older Bethel Cottage: the very earliest chapels being much simpler in form than those that followed in the 19th century.

5. Mynachdy Colliery

Dug into the side of the hill, rather than sunk deep underground like the later Lady Windsor Colliery, coal would have been excavated for local use at sites such as this long before mining on an industrial scale came to the area in the 1880s. A short diversion from the main route, turning left along the track immediately after crossing the Ffrwd, will bring you to the site. The remains of the

Mynachdy Colliery

pony stables and the old powderhouse – where explosives for blasting the rock were stored – can still be seen.

6. Mynachdy

The latter section of the walk follows an ancient pilgrimage route linking Llantarnam Abbey with the holy site of Penrhys (see walk 2), which now forms part of the Cistercian Way long-distance footpath.

Above Ynysybwl was one of Llantarnam Abbey's grange farms. Mynachdy Grange would have been used as a hosteliery both by pilgrims and by monks travelling on estate business, with the seven miles from Mynachdy via Llanwynno being the last leg in a three-day journey of 32 miles from Llantarnam to Penrhys. Modern-day Mynachdy farm is considered the most likely location for the old grange, but sadly there are no visible remains.

Cae Maen

7. Cae Maen

Though it may appear uncannily like some ancient man-made monument, this collection of large stones on the hillside overlooking Cwm Clydach and Ynysybwl is actually believed to be natural in origin, with the rocks having been carried here by the glaciers over 10,000 years ago.

Walk Directions: (-) denotes Point of Interest

Turn left out of the car park and walk uphill then turn right at the junction at the top. The churchyard (1) gate is now on your right and the grave of Guto Nyth Brân can be easily found behind the trancept to the right of the church. On leaving the churchyard by the same gate, turn right and continue along the road until you come to the entrance for Daerwynno on the right.

Turn right into the forest and follow the track. At the fork in the track, follow the main track as it turns sharply to the right and downhill (do not go through the metal barrier straight ahead). Continue along the track and through a kissing-gate into the grounds of Daerwynno Outdoor Centre. Follow the track past the main building, and then exit through the kissing-gate at the opposite end.

Cross the forestry track and follow the footpath that leads straight ahead into the woods. The path meanders through a mixed woodland for a distance of about ¾ mile / 1 km until it meets another track, at which point you should turn right. Almost immediately, the path crosses the Sychnant stream, and you should be able to hear Pistyll Goleu waterfall (2) to the left. Turn left along a narrow path to reach it via some wooden steps, before returning and continuing along the path you were on.

The path meets a single track road and continues through a metal barrier opposite. Continue to follow the same path as it broadly follows the stream. You will cross two wooden footbridges and soon after the second one there is a fork, where you should keep right. Eventually, a short incline brings you to the Perthcelyn to Llanwynno road. Cross the road, and turn right along it for a few yards. You will see a footpath heading off to the left, which you should take. Follow this path until it comes to another forestry track via some boulders. Turn left along the track and follow it first downhill then, after crossing the Nant Clydach stream, gently uphill.

About 400 metres after crossing the stream, a path heads off from the track to the left, again with boulders across it. The path is stony at first but then becomes more gravelly. Continue along the

Turn left off path to cross ditch

same path, ignoring more minor ones heading off to the left or right, until it sweeps right and starts climbing, becoming stony again for a period before becoming a metalled track. Just before the track turns sharply to the right again as it approaches the top of the hill, another path heads off to the left, over a narrow ditch and through some undergrowth, before you emerge from the woods onto an open hillside overlooking the Cynon Valley.

Turn right along the minor road and continue along it until it takes a sharp turn to the left, at which point you should continue along the rougher track which continues straight ahead. At this point there are some particularly impressive, and high, dry stone walls to your right. Continue to head in a southerly direction along this track for 1½ miles, passing through three gates on your way. During the section, you will pass the overgrown spoil tips of the Lady Windsor Colliery (3) to your right, with Ynysybwl in the valley beyond.

Shortly after the third gate, which is next to a mobile phone mast, you drop down to a small clearing. At this point, do a 'hairpin turn' and pass through a gate onto another path heading in a north-westerly direction. Follow this path for around 200 metres until you come to a path on your left heading downhill via some steps into a wood. You shortly come to a metalled track which you should cross and take the path opposite which continues downhill. You cross another path before you come to a cycle path at the bottom of the hill (which like many cycle paths in the area, follows the route of a dismantled railway). Turn left along the cycle path, and then right over a bridge which brings you to a lane. Turn left along the lane and follow it until you come to New Road. Cross the road and follow the green footpath sign which

Do a 'hairpin' turn at the clearing

Turn left along the cycle path

takes you between a house and a garage and through a kissing-gate. At first, this path may be rather overgrown and muddy but it soon broadens out before joining a minor road next to a large house. Turn right along the road and continue uphill.

You soon come to Cribyn Du farm on your left. Enter the yard near the new houses and pass between the outbuildings on your left and dog kennels on your right. Beyond the kennels, you are faced with two gates, both with green/yellow footpath signs. Take the right hand gate, and cross the field towards the far left corner where there is a stile into the next field. In this second field, follow the perimeter fence on your left until you come to a footbridge and another stile into a third field. Head across this field, bearing slightly to the right and downhill to come to a stile at the edge of a copse. The stile takes you into a fourth and final field, which may be slightly boggy to start. Ahead of you, a gate in a dry stone wall gives access to a woodland.

The path crosses the garden of Bethel Cottage

Follow the path through woods and out into a field at the other end, where you can see Bethel Cottage (4) in front of you. The path goes through the garden, to the left of the house, and down to the road. A path between the trees opposite heads down to the Ffrwd river. Having crossed the footbridge over the river, a left turn along the path which follows the river upstream will take you to the remains of Mynachdy Colliery (5).

Having retraced your steps to the main path, head away from the footbridge until the path forks, at which point you should take the left hand option that takes you uphill, out of the woods, and onto farmland. Head uphill towards the line of trees that run up the middle of the field, and follow their line until you come to a path that takes you to the right of some farm buildings and onto a single track road.

Mynachdy Farm (6) is on your right, but the route heads to the left. Eventually the track forks, at which point you should take the right hand option. Follow the track as it climbs gently uphill, with the curiosity of the Cae Maen (7) on the other side of the wall on your right. As you approach a stone wall ahead, cross the field diagonally to come to a stile at the far left corner. Continue uphill with the motorcycle track to your left until you come to another stile. Having crossed the stile, turn left along the track and into the woods. Continue along this track until you come, via a metal barrier, to a road. Turn left along the road, and just around the corner you will find Llanwynno and your start point.

Porth, Penrhys and the Rhondda Fach

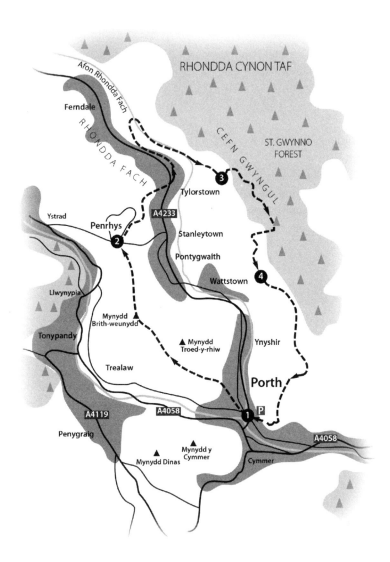

2. Porth, Penrhys and the Rhondda Fach

Approx distance: *10.5 miles / 17 km*

Approx time: *5 hours*

O.S Maps: *1: 50,000 OS Landranger Sheet 170*

1: 25,000 OS Explorer Sheet 166 (recommended)

Start: *The walk starts and ends at the Rheola Road car park in Porth. Grid Ref. ST 024 915. The post code for the start point is CF39 0LF.*

Access: *Porth stands at the meeting-point of the two Rhondda valleys, just off the main A4058 Pontypridd – Treorchy road. Rheola Road is near the town centre, and passes under the prominent Rheola Bridge. Porth train station is about 250 metres to the south, and has regular trains to Pontypridd and Cardiff, as well as northwards to Treherbert.*

Parking: *Free car park on Rheola Road. The car park is next to the Rheola Inn, but should not be confused with the pub's own car park. There is also parking at Penrhys which could be used as an alternative start and end point.*

Terrain: *Mostly along clear paths and tracks. The hillside around Tylorstown Tip and Carn y Wiwer can be boggy. Navigation around Carn y Wiwer can be tricky in poor visibility.*

Please note: *The walk has a total ascent of around 600 meters / 1,980 feet. Most of this total is divided between two sustained climbs; one at the start from Porth up to Mynydd Troed-y-rhiw and the other around the half-way mark, from Tylorstown up to Cefn Gwyngul and Tylorstown Tip.*

Facilities: *Porth has all the facilities you would expect in a small town. The Rheola Inn next to the start point serves real ale and is well worth a visit to quench your thirst after the walk.*

Points of Interest

1. Porth

Porth (literally translated – *Gateway*) is an apt name for this town which stands at the confluence of the two Rhondda rivers. Today its skyline is dominated by the striking white bridge carrying the by-pass opened in 2006, but it has been an important crossing point for many centuries; a bridge at Rheola being one of only four bridges over the Rhondda rivers mentioned in a survey of 1530.

While deep mining didn't arrive in the Rhondda until the 1850s, seams close to the surface had been mined around Porth, at Dinas and Cymmer, since the start of the 19th century. A branch of the Taff Vale Railway reached Porth in 1841, a full fifteen years before it was extended to Treorchy (*Treorci*) and Ferndale (*Glynrhedynog*) when deep mining took hold further up the two valleys.

As you climb out of Porth towards Mynydd Troed-y-rhiw, a broad view opens below you, including the vast Llethrdu cemetery at Trealaw. The cemetery is an example of the municipal cemeteries that were established during the second half of the 19th century, when population growth meant that churchyards could no longer cope with the number of burials required. The cemetery is the final resting place for over 92,000 people, including the victims of the Rhondda's last mining disaster at the Cambrian Colliery in Clydach Vale in 1965.

Just south of Porth, on the road to Pontypridd, is the Rhondda

View from the well at Penrhys

Our Lady of Penrhys

Heritage Park at Trehafod. Based at the former Taff Merthyr Colliery which closed in 1983, it provides an insight into the life of coal mining communities in the Rhondda and beyond.

2. Penrhys

A grange or manor belonging to the Cistercian Abbey at Llantarnam was located here in medieval times, with a chapel and hostelry also incorporated into the complex. Legend has it that a wooden statue of the Virgin Mary appeared in a tree near the well, and by the 15th century the shrine built to house it had become an important pilgrimage site. The shrine was burnt to the ground in 1538 at the time of Henry VIII's dissolution of the monasteries, and the statue taken to London where it too was burnt.

The well was later restored, and the small sandstone church built around it. A stone replica of the statue was erected in 1953 on the site of the old Penrhys chapel, a surviving fragment of which is incorporated into the modern boundary wall to the north of the statue.

In the early 20th century, a smallpox hospital was located here, the site having been chosen because of its remoteness from the towns and villages in the two valleys on either side. The 1960s housing estate which currently occupies the hilltop consisted originally of 1,000 units, of which only around 300 remain today.

3. Tylorstown Tip/Old Smokey

Known locally as 'Old Smokey' because of the smoke and steam which used to rise from this volcano-like structure, the tip above Tylorstown (*Pendyrys*) is the most prominent of the hill-top coal waste tips that remain in south Wales. On a clear day it is visible not only from the Brecon Beacons but also from across the Severn in Somerset and Devon; in fact, it is a regular presence on the skyline during many of the walks in this book. The view from the top is well worth the steep climb up.

The tip consists of waste material from the pits which once dotted the Rhondda Fach valley; when the industry was at its peak, Ferndale (*Glynrhedynog*) and Tylorstown alone had eight pits between them. In the past, black waste tips lined hillsides throughout south Wales, but most were removed after the Aberfan disaster in 1966.

The first deep coal mine in the Rhondda Fawr was sunk at Treherbert in 1855, with the first in the Rhondda Fach soon following at Ferndale in 1857. For the next sixty years and more, the Rhondda valleys were the most important area in the world for the production of steam coal. At its peak in 1913, there were 53 collieries in operation, producing a total of 9.85 million tonnes of

Tylorstown Tip

coal. It was exported accross the world from the docks at Cardiff, Barry and Penarth, being preferred not only by the British Navy but also by those of many foreign powers.

The unique geology of the coalfield contributed to both the size and prominence of the waste tips. The south Wales coalfield is the only mountainous one in Britain, meaning that the precious space on the valley floors was needed for pitheads, housing, roads and railways. The waste was carried up to the hillsides out of the way. At the same time, the nature of the coal seams: deep underground, folded and split out of shape over the millennia, and alternating with layers of shale, sandstone and other rocks, meant that there was more waste per ton of coal produced in south Wales than in other coalfields.

The last mine in the Rhondda, in Maerdy at the head of the Rhondda Fach, closed in 1990.

House Platforms Carn y Wiwer

Rhondda Heritage Park

4. Carn y Wiwer

The hillside at Carn y Wiwer not only provides spectacular views over the Rhondda Fach from Tylorstown to Porth, but is also a site of considerable historical interest.

Around twenty Bronze Age cairns are found in the area, the most prominent of which is near the top of the ridge at grid reference ST 027 941. There are also two pairs of medieval house platforms (at ST 027 939 and ST 026 940) where early farmers would have lived, possibly on a seasonal basis. Set at right angles to the hillside, the houses would have been rudimentary structures built of stone and turf, possibly with a thatched roof. The farmer's family lived at one end, while cattle were housed at the other.

There is also evidence of historical ploughing in the area, though there is some uncertainty as to whether it is contemporary with the platform houses or later in date. One suggestion is that the hillside was cultivated to alleviate food shortages during the Napoleonic wars of the late 18th and early 19th centuries.

Walk Directions: (-) denotes Point of Interest

From the Rheola Road car park in Porth (1), turn right past the pub and under the bridge. Continue to the mini roundabout, where you need to take the steps that climb to the left of the road ahead. Continue along Troed-y-rhiw Road until you come to the gate of Troed-y-rhiw Farm. Go through the gate and, keeping to the right of the farm buildings, pick up the old parish road.

Exit the farmyard via the gate and cross a stream. Continue along the track as it climbs uphill, including one particularly steep and stony section. Keep left at the fork at the top of the hill to pass through a gate and then to the right of a mast. Ahead you will see a stile that leads onto a golf course. Cross the golf course, sticking

Keep left at the fork

to the track throughout, until you get to the clubhouse. On the way you will pass a trigpoint marking the summit of Mynydd Brith-weunydd, though it is easily missed among the greens and bunkers.

Looking ahead from the clubhouse, the Ffynnon Fair well can be clearly seen on the left of the access road, with the Lady of Penrhys (2) statue above it on the right of the road. Continue along the road, and you will come to a path leading down to the well shortly after you pass the beacon on your left. From the well, retrace your steps to the road and cross it to continue uphill until you get to the statue. Pass through the boundary wall and

A footpath from the lay-by

carefully cross the busy road in front of the Penrhys housing estate. Keeping the cemetery on your right, follow the road that climbs uphill around the estate's perimeter, and turn right at the juction next to the primary school. Follow this road as it sweeps left, and then starts climbing uphill. About half way up the hill a footpath leads off from a lay-by on the right. Take this path, and where it forks take the right-hand option, heading downhill and keeping the woods on your left.

After a short distance you come to a metalled road – turn left along it. When you come to the boulders at its junction with another road, cross that road and head along the path with a handrail which is to the left of the wall in front of you. Continue down a series of steps, crossing each street you come to, until at the end of Prospect Place you come to some lockup garages.

Pass to the left of the garages and turn left along the path behind them. Pass to the right of the leisure centre and past the miners' memorial. About 100 meters later the path forks and you should keep right to head downhill and join a cycle path on the river bank. Turn left along the cycle path and then, some time later, right over the wooden footbridge. Turn left on the other side of the bridge so that the river is now on your left. After a little less than half a mile, a gravelly path heads off to the right through the woods. It is easy to miss, so if you come to a concrete grit bin on your right, you need to go back about 50 meters. The path bends sharply right and is flat for a period before starting

A gravelly path on the right

to climb steadily. Continue to follow the path uphill towards the obvious target of Tylorstown Tip (3) up ahead. From the foot of the tip, don't take the steep direct route up the tip used by bikes, but rather the path that follows a curving ditch just to the left of the bike tracks.

Having taken some time to admire the views, and a well-earned rest, return down the same path. At the bottom, turn right to come to a gravelly clearing, which you should cross heading away from the tip. Turn left at the junction of paths to come to the mountain road. Turn right along it for about 200 meters, and then take the forestry track that heads off it to the right. After a little over half a mile, the track meets another at a T-junction via a wall of boulders, and you should turn right. The track climbs a little out of the woods before starting to descend, at which point another track heads off to the left.

Follow this track for around 400 meters until it passes through old gateposts. At this point, take the less distinct grassy path that heads off half-right. This path soon disappears completely, but you should continue across the hillside in the same southerly direction, losing height gradually. You are now crossing the Carn y Wiwer cairnfield (4), and your direction of

A grassy path half-right

travel should bring you naturally to the platform houses. This section of the walk has fantastic views of the Rhondda Fach valley from Penrhys in the north to Porth in the south, with Pontygwaith and Wattstown (*Aberllechau*) on the valley floor in between.

From the platform houses, contour along the hillside (do not drop down any further) until you come to another track running parallel to an old fence. Pass through one of the gaps in the fence and head uphill to the top right-hand corner of the large field ahead. At the field corner, cross the stile next to a white post then pass between two dry stone walls to come to another stile. Continue along the ridge, keeping close to the fence on your right, until you come to another stile at the far end of the field. Cross the stile and turn left so that the wall is now on your left and continue in the same direction, past a trig point in the adjoining field, and then over another stile. Here two dry stone walls head off at different angles each side of you – follow the one on your left.

Pass through the gate then turn right along the track which heads downhill. Where this track bends left, turn right through the large metal gate with a bridleway waymark. At the next fork, turn left to pass through yet another gate.

Continue along this track, passing a mast on your right. Where the track becomes a metalled road and turns sharply left towards a farm, you should take the narrow path heading downhill to your right. When you come to the entrance gate to the waterworks, turn right along the access road and then right again at the bottom of the hill. Follow the streets downhill to return to your start point underneath the Rheola Bridge.

Mynydd Cilfach yr Encil from Parc Taf Bargoed

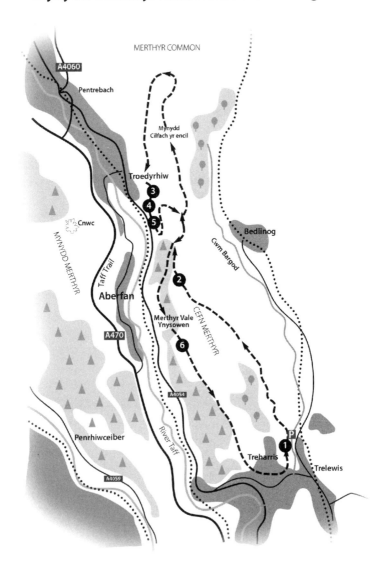

3. Mynydd Cilfach yr Encil from Parc Taf Bargoed

Approx distance: 11.5 miles / 18.5 km. As this walk takes the form of a 'figure of 8', there is the option of splitting the walk in two and doing only half at a time.

Approx time: 5.5 hours

O.S Maps: 1: 50,000 OS Landranger Sheet 170 & 171
1: 25,000 OS Explorer Sheet 166 (recommended)

Start: The walk starts and ends at the pavilion building in Parc Taf Bargoed. Grid reference: ST 102 976. Post code: CF46 6RD

Access: From the A470 or from Nelson, follow the signs for the climbing centre until you get to Trelewis. As you head out of Trelewis in the direction of the climbing centre and Bedlinog, the entrance to Parc Taf Bargoed is on the left after the last house on the High Street.

Parking: Opposite the pavilion building, from where the walk starts. There is also parking on the lakeside – turn right along the track after the pavilion. For those wishing to split the walk and only do the northernmost loop, there is a small lay-by close to where the loops meet, near the entrance to Merthyr and Gelligaer Common.

Terrain: Mostly along clear paths, tracks and minor roads. The section above Troedyrhiw can be quite muddy in places, while the Rhiw Gymrwg is a track of loose stones that requires a little care.

Please note: The walk has a total ascent of around 550m / 1,650 feet, most of which is gentle. There are,

	however, three moderately steep sections in the second half of the walk which some may find hard going on top of the mileage already covered.
Facilities:	*There are public toilets in the Parc Taf Bargoed pavilion, while snacks are available from a cabin next to the lake. Both Trelewis and Treharris have convenience stores etc, while the Glan Taff Inn at Quaker's Yard serves food and real ale and is recommended for post-walk refreshments.*

Points of Interest

1. Parc Taf Bargoed

Taking in the sites of three old collieries: Deep Navigation, Taff Merthyr and Trelewis Drift, Parc Taf Bargoed is possibly the finest example in the valleys of the transformation of an old industrial site. Just twenty years ago, a visitor to this spot would have found a vast industrial site, and the river hidden from view. Today, wildlife flourishes in the woods and lakes, and the park provides opportunities for all kinds of recreational and sporting activities, including one of Britain's highest indoor climbing walls.

The Deep Navigation Colliery stood where the pavilion building now is. First sunk by the Harris Navigation Steam Coal Company in 1873 (that in turn gave its name to Treharris) the 760 yard shaft was at the time the deepest in the whole coalfield. The mine produced some of the finest quality steam coal in the world, and powered the Cunard steamers *RMS Mauretania* and *RMS Lusitania* as they set new speed records for crossing the Atlantic. Coal from Deep Naviagtion also fuelled the Titanic. Often at the forefront of innovation, it was one of the first mines to have shafts wound by electricity, and in 1933 became the first in south Wales

Parc Taf Bargoed

to have pit-head baths. It closed on Good Friday 1991.

Taff Merthyr Colliery, operational from 1924–1993, was located where the climbing centre now stands, at the northern end of the park. It was one of the last to be sunk under private ownership, and found itself at the forefront of the industrial disputes of the 1930s. In October 1935, a fierce battle was fought between supporters of the striking South Wales Miners Fedaration (the 'Fed') on the one side, and the South Wales Miners Industrial Union (SWMIU – the 'company' or blackleg union) on the other. The battle started underground then spread to the surface, with stones being thrown and fighting on the hillsides, leaving forty people injured. In the biggest trial of its kind seen in Britain, 53 men and 3 women were sentenced for up to 15 months imprisonment, as the government sought to crack down on such industrial action by mine workers during the depression.

Forest Chapel

2. Forest Chapel

Lying in a shallow saddle on Mynydd y Capel are the remains of a medieval building comprising of four exterior walls and a small yard. Traditionally believed to be a chapel, recent inspections have suggested it is more likely to be of agricultural origin.

To its south, on the plateau of Mynydd y Capel, are least 81 Bronze Age cairns. Together with the track which you have been walking along, which follows the ancient ridgeway route along the mountain, these features are a reminder that it is only in relatively-modern times that that the valleys have superceeded the hills as the focus of human habitation in south Wales.

3. Mount Pleasant

In the post-industrial landscape of the Merthyr Tydfil area, this grassy mound could easily be mistaken for one of the overgrown spoil tips that dot the area. This particular hillock, however, is of natural origin and is made up of the debris from an ancient landslip that left the scar of Craig y Pwll on the hillside above.

4. Troedyrhiw Lido

The land and materials for the lido were donated in 1934 by Patrick Wyndham Murray Threipland, a Cardiff-based landowner with land in the area, and whose wife wished to do something to help the residents of Troedyrhiw during the difficult times of the depression. The actual construction was undertaken by local men, many of whom would have been unemployed and suffereing considerable hardship at the time, and its completion was celebrated with an official opening ceremony in 1935 that included swimming competitions for local children.

Sadly, the lido has been disused for many decades, but its spectacular setting can still be appreciated. Though the lido itself

Craig y Pwll and Troedyrhiw Lido

Looking towards Merthyr Tydfil from Rhiw Gymrwg

wasn't constructed until the 1930s, some kind of natural pool had already existed on the same site, and may explain the name of the Craig y Pwll cliffs which rise behind it.

5. Rhiw Gymrwg

The Rhiw Gymrwg is part of an old route that linked the area's dispersed farms long before the modern-day towns and villages were built. In fact, it is the Rhiw Gymrwg that puts the 'rhiw' in Troedyrhiw (literally, *foot of the slope*): the nearest village to you in the valley below.

In pre-industrial times, there stood two farms at each end of the 'rhiw': Pen y Rhiw Gymrwg at the top and Troed y Rhiw Gymrwg at the bottom, which subsequently gave its name to the village that grew up around it in the 19th century. The ruins of the old farmhouse stood until 1967, when a school was built on the site.

In recent years, the track has become popular with trial motorcyclists, one of whom has his achievements commemorated on a large stone along the route.

6. View of Aberfan
Aberfan is visited in walk 9. However, this vantage point on the opposite side of the valley to it provides an opportunity to understand the geography of the 1966 tragedy. The Pantglas Primary school was located at the northern end of the village, and the footprint of the tips that towered above it can still be seen on the hillside just to the north-west. Streams can be seen running down the hillside from the area where the tips stood; these were a key contributing factor to their instability.

Walk Directions: (-) denotes Point of Interest
With the Parc Taf Bargoed (1) pavilion on your left, head up the minor road straight ahead which climbs gradually towards Mynydd y Capel. After a mile or so, you come to Tirlan Farm. Take the path to the left of the farm entrance. Cross another stile into a walled enclosure and turn left along the track which eventually takes you through another gate onto open hillside.

Continue to follow the same track in a generally northwards direction, keeping right at the fork next to the upright marker stone. Soon after passing the remains of Forest Chapel on your right (2), you start losing height and pass through a gate, then come to a minor road next to a cattle grid (you will return to this point later on in the walk). Turn right along the road until you enter Merthyr and Gelligaer Common over another cattle grid.

At this point, turn right off the road and follow the fence on your right until you pick up a track running along the top of the

Follow the fence on the right

escarpment, with the village of Bedlinog below you on your right. Follow the track northwards, and soon the top of Mynydd Cilfach yr Encil comes into view ahead. The path becomes less distinct, and you should cross the mountain track to pick up a clearer path that leads to the summit itself. From the top, continue northwards at first, then bear right as you drop down from the summit to regain the mountain track road and follow it as it sweeps leftwards and downhill. When the road starts to swing back to the right, leave it to the left and pass between patches of rushes to pick up a grassy track heading southwards. From here, fine views open up of Merthyr Tydfil (*Merthyr Tudful*) and the Taff valley below.

Continue along this track, with the escarpment of Mynydd Cilfach yr Encil above you on your left. Pass through a gate and continue straight ahead. The path becomes less distinct and muddier as it meanders between trees and patches of undergrowth. The cliffs of Craig y Pwll are ahead on the left, and you can see the mound of Mount Pleasant (3) which stands at the foot of the cliffs, with a clear track running up it – the path you are following bears right and drops down a little to bring you to the foot of this mound. Climb it and then descend the other side towards the old lido (4). The path passes to the right of the lido and soon starts to climb again – gently at first and then more steeply as you join the stony track of Rhiw Gymrwg (5).

At the top of the climb, as the path becomes grassier and levels out, you come to a stone wall and fence. You need to turn left and follow the line of the wall. Depending on the time of year, and the thickness of the bracken, you may find the best path either just below the wall or between the wall and the fence. Whichever path you follow, you eventually come to a corner where the wall and fence turn sharply right and head uphill. You should do likewise, keeping the wall on your right, until you come to a small metal gate at the top of the hill.

Pass through the gate and turn right, picking up a grassy track that brings you back to the cattle grid where you entered the common. Retrace your steps along the road to a second cattle grid and continue along the road as it passes through some woods. Where the woods end on the left hand side, turn left off the road, following a stone wall to come to a stile. Cross the stile and continue along the grassy track uphill towards the TV mast. This section gives great views of the villages of Aberfan (6) and Merthyr Vale (*Ynysowen*) in the valley below.

Just before the mast, the track turns sharp left and then right to bring you to the crest of the ridge. Turn right and head southwards, passing to the left of the mast and through a gate onto another minor road. Follow this road for a little over a mile / 1.5 km until you come down a steep hill into Treharris.

At the bottom of the hill, next to the church, turn left along Bargoed Terrace. Where the road forks at the Navigation Hotel / The Navi, take the right-hand option. Soon you will see Railway Terrace on your left. At the far end of the terrace is an entrance to Parc Taf Bargoed. Once in the park, turn right over the bridge and then left to bring you back to the start point.

Gelligaer Common and Cefn Brithdir

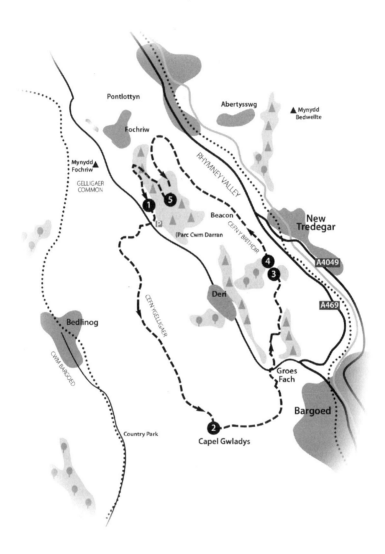

Pontlottyn

Abertysswg

▲ Mynydd Bedwellte

Fochriw

Mynydd ▲ Fochriw

GELLIGAER COMMON

RHYMNEY VALLEY

1

5

Beacon

CEFN Y BRITHDIR

New Tredegar

(Parc Cwm Darran)

4

A4049

3

Deri

A469

CEFN Y GELLIGAER

Bedlinog

CWM BARGOED

Groes Fach

Bargoed

2

Country Park

Capel Gwladys

4. Gelligaer Common and Cefn Brithdir

Approx distance: 11 miles / 17.5 km
Approx time: 5.5 hours
O.S Maps: 1: 50,000 OS Landranger Sheet 171
1: 25,000 OS Explorer Sheet 166 (recommended)
Start & End: The walk starts and ends at Parc Cwm Darran between Deri and Fochriw in the Darran Valley.
Access: Parc Cwm Darran is signposted from the A468 at Bargoed, two miles to the south. The park entrance is on the right hand side of the road half way between Deri and Fochriw. The Darran Valley cycleway from Bargoed to Fochriw passes through the park, while the Bargoed to Merthyr Tydfil (no. 1) and Bargoed to Tredegar (no. 4) buses stop outside the park.
Parking: At Parc Cwm Darran.
Terrain: A mixture of open country, tracks, paths, and roadside walking. Much of the second half of the walk follows the route of Rhymney Ridgeway long distance path.
Please note: The walk has a moderate total ascent and descent of 500 meters / 1,550 feet. Most of the climbing takes place over two stretches: at the start of the walk as you climb from Parc Cwm Darran onto Gelligaer Common, and then at around half-way as you climb from Groes-faen onto the Cefn Brithdir ridge.
Facilities: Parc Cwm Darran visitor centre has a cafe and toilets.

Parc Cwm Darran

Capel Gwladys

Points of Interest

1. Parc Cwm Darran

Like its counterpart Parc Taf Bargoed on the other side of Gelligaer Common (see walk 3), Parc Cwm Darran is a spectacular example of nature's ability to reclaim former industrial sites.

The park was previously occupied by the Oglivie Colliery and its spoil tips. Operational between 1920 and 1975, the Oglivie employed up to 1,500 people at its peak, and was the largest mine in the Darran Valley. It was also the location for the filming of the Dr Who episode 'The Green Death' in 1973.

Today, the park has numerous attractions for the visitor, including Oglivie Lake with its twenty fishing platforms, numerous picnic areas, and an open air amphitheatre. The Cwmllwydrew Meadows Local Nature Reserve provides a haven for toads, newts and pied flycatchers – a short trail gives visitors access to the meadows. Meanwhile, a surviving relic from the Oglivie Colliery is the restored powder store: one of the few still standing in Wales.

2. Capel Gwladys

The remains of Capel Gwladys, marked today by a low stone wall and Celtic cross, date back to the 5th century. To the north and west of the chapel are the remains of an earthwork enclosure, which may mark the boundary of the land that once belonged to it. In 1906, a decorated and inscribed stone cross from the 8th century was discovered here. It can now be seen in Gelligaer parish church two miles away.

Saint Gwladys herself was the eldest daughter of the Welsh king Brychan Brycheiniog, whose kingdom lay to the north, and she led a tumultuous life. She was wanted for marriage by Gwynllyw, a local warrior king, but her father would not consent. And so Gwynllyw led an army of 300 men north to Talgarth to kidnap her. He was pursued back south by Brychan and his men as far as modern-day Fochriw, where a pitched battle was fought. Legend has is that the battle was settled in Gwynllyw's favour when King Arthur himself intervened on his side.

Under the influence of Gwladys, and their son Cattwg Ddoeth (Saint Cadog the Wise), Gwynllyw eventually gave up his warring ways and established a hermitage in Newport (*Casnewydd*), where he is celebrated as the city's founder. Gwladys herself established her own hermitages, firstly at Pont Ebbw in modern-day Bassaleg, and then here on Cefn Gelligaer.

3. Capel y Brithdir

Unlike Capel Gwladys, Capel y Brithdir is modern in origin. Built in the 16th Century as a chapel of ease for the parish church at Gelligaer,

Rhymney Valley View

it allowed the inhabitants of this part of the parish easier access to a place of worship. While its location today may seem remote, at that time (and indeed a millenium earlier, when the Tegernacus stone was erected) the Cefn y Brithdir ridgeway track would have been the key communication route in this sparsely populated area.

The chapel fell out of use during the 19th century as new churches were built to serve the fast-growing populations of the mining villages in both the Rhymney (*Rhymni*) and Darran valleys. A visitor in 1862 described the chapel as 'a small chapel frequented apparently by but few persons besides the clergyman and his clerk; and having a rotten wooden belfry, but no bell, the bell having been stolen...' When the chapel was demolished in 1960, a cross incised slab dating to the end of the first millenium was found in its walls. The slab is now in St Gwladys's Church, Bargoed. The inscriptions on the graves remind us that the chapel served an overwhelmingly Welsh-speaking population, and it is in Welsh that its services were conducted.

4. Tegernacus Stone

Standing just to the west of the ancient ridgeway along Cefn Brithdir is the site of the Tegernacus Stone, a roughly-cut slab about 2.25 meters high and 1 meter wide. The stone was relocated to the National Museum for Wales in 1923, and was replaced by the concrete pillar visible today.

The stone bore the inscription TEGERNACUS FILIUS MARTI HIC IACIT (Tegernacus, son of Martius, lies here) carved vertically across four lines in a Roman style. The identity of Tegernacus is not known, though some have suggested he may be Tyrnon, grandson of Gwladys, and the same Tegernacus who is cited as 'father of Cadog' on another inscribed stone at Cwmdu, Brecknockshire.

5. Brithdir Uchaf

Standing at a junction of tracks surrounded by forestry, the ruins of Brithdir Uchaf can catch the unsuspecting walker by surprise. Whilst abandoned and ruined farms are found on every hillside throughout the valleys, there is something particularly haunting about Brithdir Uchaf.

Perhaps it is because the outline of the 17th century range house and cowhouse is so complete, allowing the visitor to wander through the doorways from room to room in the footsteps of those who once lived and farmed here. The stone walls that would have marked the boundaries of its fields and

Brithdir Uchaf

enclosures can also still be seen among the trees of the plantation which has engulfed it, while the tracks the walker follows are the same ones as the inhabitants would themselves have travelled as they went about their business.

A survey of 1841 shows the farm comprising of 156 acres, making it one of the most substantial in the district. Soon after, Brithdir Uchaf was caught up in the transformation of the Darran valley from rural tranquility to industrial heartland. While much of the surrounding land was owned by the Marquess of Bute, Brithdir Uchaf and some other neighbouring farms were not. And so, in 1885, when the Dowlais Iron Company was negotiating a lease to extract coal from the seams below the Cefn Brithdir ridge, a meeting was held at Brithdir Uchaf between the representatives of the Company, the landowners, and the Bute Estate to negotiate the terms of the lease: the Bute representative having come on horseback over Gelligaer Common from the nearest railway station at Bedlinog. Brithdir Uchaf and its surrounds would never be the same again.

Walk Directions: (-) denotes Point of Interest

Trail indicated by bridleway fingerpoint

From Parc Cwm Darran (1), head uphill along the access road to the main road. Turn right along the road and continue for about 100 meters until, on the opposite side of the road, a track climbs away from the road towards a wooden gate. The track is indicated by a bridleway fingerpost. Cross the road and follow this track through a pair of gates, and then continue along it to another gate giving access to a field. Walk uphill through the field, following the line of trees to come to another pair of gates at the top right corner of the field.

On the other side of the gates, the path forks. Take the left hand option uphill, and then at the crossroads of paths continue straight ahead to come to a junction of mountain roads. Follow the road straight ahead until you come to a lay-by, where you should turn left off the road and follow a grassy track heading south across the common between patches of rushes. (To the right (north) of the lay-by, and worth a short detour, are Carn y Bugail and the Carreg Fain-hir Standing Stone described in Walk 8.)

The grassy track broadens out before crossing a minor road at a row of boulders and then climbing slightly. Pass under the power cables as the path levels out again, before coming to the mountain road at an upright marker stone. Cross the road and continue to follow the track on the other side, with the road now to your right. Following a short incline, the track then descends slowly, crossing yet another minor road, before passing a lay-by marked by boulders on your right.

Shortly after the lay-by, a clear path leads through the gorse and bracken to your left (it is indicated by a fingerpost on the other side of the road on your right). Turn left along this path, and follow it as it crosses an area of unenclosed grassland and through the line of an old dyke to arrive at Capel Gwladys (2), marked by a Celtic cross.

From the monument, head to the road and turn left along it. You are now following the route of the Rhymney Ridgeway path. Continue along the road until you come to a left hand turn just before the school. Cross the cattle grid then turn immediately right through the green metal barrier. Follow the track until it turns sharply left towards Pencaedrain Farm. At this point, continue straight ahead through the wooden gate and follow the path downhill. Having entered a woodland, take the left hand option where the path forks. Continue over the footbridge then along the riverbank for a short distance, before passing under a stone arch bridge and heading away from the river. Turn left at the Caradog's Bridge boulder, to head uphill along a track of black gravel to come to the main road at Groes-faen.

Cross the road and head up the track on the left before the terrace, up the steps to the left then through a wooden bridleway gate. Continue up the farm track until you come to another wooden gate on the left just before the farmyard. Pass through the gate and continue uphill, taking the right hand fork in the path (do not go over the stile) to pass through yet another wooden gate. Take the track straight ahead, passing through two more gates, and continuing to follow the track as it bears right then right again as it follows the field boundary on your left. Regular blue bridleway waymarkers help remove any doubt during this section. Shortly after the point where the wall becomes a metal fence, pass through a gate on your left.

Take right hand fork to stream

The track remains clear as it enters an area of sparse woodland, where it eventually forks. You need to take the right hand fork that leads to the Nant Llan stream and crosses it. (If you come to a large metal gate, with no stile or waymark, you have passed the fork and need to go back about 50 meters.)

Having crossed the stream, pass through the gate and continue uphill past Ty'r Capel farm on your left. At the top of the hill, turn left and continue to find Capel y Brithdir (3) on your right, followed shortly by the Tegernacus Stone (4) on your left.

Continue along the same track for around two miles as it crosses open moorland with great views of the Rhymney valley on your right and the Brecon Beacons to the north. Eventually the track drops down substantially, sweeping to the left as it does so, with a conifer plantation coming into view straight ahead. Where the track bends right again, a less distinct path heads off it to the left. Follow this track for about half a mile until it enters the forest through gateposts.

Continue along the track, until you come to the ruins of Brithdir Uchaf (5). Here, turn sharply right and downhill. You soon come to a clearing, where you should take the grassy path heading down half left from the main forestry track, to continue downhill in the same direction as you were already heading. After about half a mile you emerge out of the forest and join a cycle path just to the south of Fochriw. Turn left and follow it back to your start point at Parc Cwm Darran.

Path continues downhill on left

Pontypridd, Senghenydd and Mynydd Eglwysilan

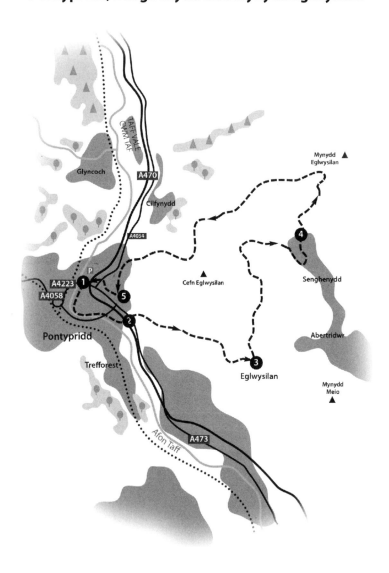

5. Pontypridd, Senghenydd and Mynydd Eglwysilan

Approx distance: *11 miles / 17.5 km*

Approx time: *5.5 hours*

O.S Maps: *1: 50,000 OS Landranger Sheet 171*

1: 25,000 OS Explorer Sheet 166 (recommended)

Start & End: *The walk starts and ends outside the Pontypridd Museum, next to the old bridge.*

Access: *Pontypridd lies just off the A470 trunk road between Cardiff and Merthyr Tydfil, and at the junction of three railway lines, making it easily accessible from Cardiff, Aberdare, Merthyr Tydfil and the Rhondda.*

The Pontypridd Museum and old bridge are in the centre of town, next to the bus station, and about 500 meters north of the railway station.

Parking: *There is a car park just to the south of the Pontypridd Museum on Taff Street, and another just behind the bus station on Chapel Street.*

Terrain: *A mixture of tracks and paths across farmland and open hillside, with some roadside walking in Pontypridd and Senghenydd.*

Please note: *The walk has a moderate total ascent and descent of about 450 meters / 1,485 feet, none of which is overly strenuous. Some sections of the walk are across farmland, and the route passes two farms, so dogs will occasionally need to be on a lead. Following periods of rain, some sections can get quite muddy, and some basic navigation skills might be required on Eglwysilan Common in poor visibility.*

Facilities: *Pontypridd is a market town with all the facilities you would expect. There are toilets at the Pontypridd Museum and at the Aber Valley Heritage Centre in Senghenydd. You might also find the Rose and Crown pub next to the church in Eglwysilan convenient.*

Points of Interest

1. Pontypridd

Originally Pont-y-tŷ-pridd (*the bridge of the earthen house*), there has existed a crossing point over the Taff (*Taf*) at this point for many centuries; the river being initially crossed via either a ford or wooden bridge, until William Edwards was commissioned in 1746 to build a permanent stone structure.

A self-taught stonemason from Eglwysilan, Edwards was only 27 when he first undertook the task for which he was paid £500 on condition that he maintained the bridge for seven years. His first attempt – a traditional three-arch bridge – lasted just two years before it was destroyed by a build-up of debris following a storm. To replace it, he decided on an ambitious single-arch structure which would be less vulnerable to being destroyed by flood. His first two attempts at such a bridge collapsed due to faults in the design, and it was then that Edwards came upon the radical solution of incorporating three holes on either side to better balance the weight across the bridge.

The resulting masterpiece was completed in 1756, and at 43 meters wide it was the longest single arch bridge in Britain, if not Europe, at the time. The iconic bridge stands to this day, though its surroundings have changed beyond all recognition. For the first half century of its existence, the bridge stood in splendid rural

Pontypridd Old Bridge

isolation, and was painted by many landscape artists, including
Julius Ibbertson and RMW Turner. In 1803, B. H Malkin described
the combination of the bridge and its setting as 'an instance
scarcely to be paralleled, of art happily introduced among the
wildest scenes of nature'.

The opening of the Glamorganshire Canal from Cardiff to
Merthyr Tydfil in 1794 made the lower Taff valley ripe for
development, and the Crawshays of Cyfarthfa established a
tinplate works at Trefforest as early as 1794. It wasn't until 1816
that industry on a major scale first arrived in Pontypridd (then
commonly known as Newbridge) however, with the
establishment of the Brown Lennox chain and anchor works. The
works supplied the Navy with chains and anchors throughout the
19th century, as well as providing the chains for many of the
suspension bridges constructed in Britain during that period,

including Telford's bridge over the Menai and Brunel's Clifton Suspension Bridge. Other industry soon followed, but the town's population was still only 2,000 in 1830.

It was the opening of the Taff Valley railway in 1840 and the extention of the branches into the two Rhondda valleys in the 1850s as those valleys became the most important steam coal production centre in the world during the latter half of the 19th century, that saw Pontypridd become the major market town of upper Glamorgan. By 1857, William Edwards' bridge was no longer fit for purpose, and the newer 'Victoria Bridge' was built next to it. Pontypridd became a gateway to the central valleys, and by 1913 an incredible 500 trains per day passed through the town's station; the longest railway platform in the world was needed in order to cope with the traffic, and it still stands today. By 1920, the town had a population approaching 50,000.

Pontypridd Museum is housed in the converted Tabernacl Chapel right next to the old bridge. It has a wide range of exhibits relating to the town's social, industrial and cultural history, and is well worth a visit.

2. Dr William Price's Roundhouses

Dr Price's life story has filled books in itself: he was one of the most colourful, eccentric, radical, controversial and visionary Welshmen that has ever lived. His long life spanned a period when Wales and Britain were undergoing huge social and cultural changes and his long life was both influenced by, and had an impact on, a range of the issues of the day.

A qualified surgeon, Dr Price (1800–1893) came originally from Rudry, Caerphilly, but spent much of his life living in and around Pontypridd, where he was company physician both at Lennox and Brown's Chain and Anchor Works and Crawshay's Trefforest Iron and Tin Works. He also had a personal practice that was highly regarded throughout the area.

In many ways, he was a visionary. He practised socialised healthcare by charging patients according to their ability to pay, and a form of health insurance by setting up a scheme whereby workers paid for his services before they became ill. He refused to treat smokers, didn't eat meat, and advocated 'free love', claiming that marriage was tantamout to the enslavery of women. While he mixed in the highest social circles – enjoying the company and patronage of, among

Roundhouse

others, the Crawshay and Guest ironmaster families – he was also a political radical, an advocate of workers' rights, and a Chartist leader. He spent a period in exile in France following the failed Chartist uprising and march on Newport in 1839.

Later in life, he moved to Llantrisant. In his 80s, he fathered three children with his housemaid who was sixty years his junior. It was in Llantrisant that he carried out his most infamous act by cremating the body of his infant son (who he had named Iesu Grist) on a hilltop outside the town in 1884. At the time, cremation was generally believed to be illegal in Britain, and he had to be protected by police to prevent his lynching by outraged locals. But his acquital at a subsequent trial established the legality of cremation and paved the way for the Cremation Act of 1902. Ironically, Glyntaff Crematorium now stands only a few meters from his former home and surgery, while his statue commands the centre of Llantrisant, where he died aged 93 sipping a glass of champagne.

Throughout his life, Dr Price was also a passionate Welsh nationalist and a prominent member of the Druidic movement which had taken root in Pontypridd (see 5 below), believing himself to be an Arch-priest of the Druidic religion. The roundhouses are relics of a project he embarked on in 1858 to build a museum for Welsh folklore and culture, a centre for Druidism, and a school for the orphaned poor on a site between his then home and the Rocking Stone. The roundhouses were built first, with the intention that they would flank a gateway leading to an imposing eight storey 'palace' behind them.

Sadly, the project was never completed, in part due to a typically relaxed attitude to the letter of the law on Price's behalf. He had leased the land from Lord and Lady Llanover (*Gwenynen Gwent*), with whom he had a long-established friendship based on their shared passion for Welsh culture. However, under the terms of the lease, Dr Price had no right to build so extensively on the land, which included valuable mineral rights and on which the Llanovers intended to lay a railway to a nearby colliery. As a result, Dr Price was evicted from the land before his vision could be fulfilled, and Wales would have to wait until 1946 for a national folk museum to be established at St Fagan (*Sain Ffagan*) near Cardiff.

3. Eglwysilan

The parish of Eglwysilan itself was created in the 12th century, and the current church building dates from that period, though it has been much restored over the intervening years. However, the church stands on the site of a much older monastic cell or chapel called Merthyr Ilan. Evidence of early Christian activity is found inside the church in the form of a stone slab containing a carving of a male figure holding a shield. Found in 1904, it is believed to date from between the 8th and 10th centuries. During the middle

Eglwysilan Church

ages, Eglwysilan was one of the stops on the important
pilgrimage route from Llantarnam to Penrhys.

Features of interest in the churchyard include the grave of
William Edwards just to the left of the porch. It was he who built
the bridge at Pontypridd (see 1 above), and he put his
stonemason skills to use by contributing to the renovation of the
church. There are also around thirty graves of the victims of the
Senghenydd Disaster of 1913 (see 4 below). The bodies were
carried up the mountain from Senghenydd in corteges a mile long
to be buried here at the parish church.

4. Senghenydd

Senghenydd was the name given to that part of the medieval
Welsh kingdom of Morgannwg which lay between the Taff (*Taf*)
and Rhymney (*Rhymni*) rivers. While the Normans had seized

Senghenydd Memorial

control of the lower parts of that kingdom by the 12th century, the upland parts remained in Welsh hands. The most famous of the Welsh leaders of Senghenydd from that time is Ifor Bach (*Ivor the Short*) who held out against the Normans from his base at Castell Coch. Most famously, in 1158 he climbed the walls of Cardiff Castle and kidnapped the Norman Lord William Fitz Robert, his wife, and son, and held them hostage until his lands were returned to him. Clwb Ifor Bach, opposite Cardiff Castle, is named in his honour.

The village of Senghenydd in the Aber valley developed around the Universal Colliery which was sunk in 1891. That colliery was the scene of two major disasters; the first in 1901 killed 81 people, and the owner William Thomas Lewis (later Lord Merthyr) was criticised by the Mining Inspectorate for a disregard for safety as he sought to sink the mine deeper and deeper. Incredibly, many of the improvements demanded in the wake of that explosion were still outstanding in October 1913, when a second explosion 650 yards underground killed 440 men and boys – the worst industrial disaster ever in Britain.

Rescue teams, including volunteer miners from surrounding collieries, worked day and night to search for survivors and recover bodies, but such was the ferocity of the blast and resulting underground inferno that they were constantly pushed back in their efforts. Apart from eighteen miners found together the following day, survivors were few and far between, and it took over a month to bury all the dead.

The disaster of 1913 left 205 widows and 542 orphaned children. With the colliery being a relatively new one, many of the victims had moved to the area only recently, mostly from other parts of Wales and neighbouring counties of England. As a result, the disaster was a national one as much as a local one. For example, many families in the quarrying villages in north-west Wales lost sons and brothers who had moved to find work in the collieries following a downturn in the slate industry in the early years of the 20th century.

In October 2013, on the centenary of the disaster, two memorials were unveiled on the former pit site. The Senghenydd Memorial comprises a bronze statue of two miners, one leading the other to safety, surrounded by a wall bearing a tile for each victim of the 1903 and 1913 disasters. The National Mining Memorial is dedicated to the memory of those lost in a total of 150 Welsh mining disasters over the years.

Those wanting to learn more about the disaster, and about the history of the area, should visit the Aber Valley Heritage Centre on Gwern Avenue.

5. The Rocking Stone (Y Maen Chwyf/Y Garreg Siglo)

Gorsedd Beirdd Ynys Prydain (*The Gorsedd of Bards of the Isle of Britain*) was established by Iolo Morganwg (Edward Williams, 1747–1826) on Primrose Hill in London in 1792. Iolo returned to Wales three years later, and the first Gorsedd at Pontypridd was held in 1815 at the Rocking Stone, which the Druids referred to as Y Maen Chwyf. For the century that followed, the neo-Druidic movement grew deep roots in Pontypridd and in Glamorgan more generally, with Y Maen Chwyf serving as a focal point for the Gorsedd's rituals and ceremonies.

Pontypridd Stone Circle

Prominent members of the Pontypridd Druidic society in the 19th century included Iolo's son *Taliesin ab Iolo* (Taliesin Williams, 1787–1847), *Myfyr Morgannwg* (Evan Davies, 1801–1888), *Morien* (Owen Morgan, 1836–1921) and Dr William Price (see 2 above). The Maen Chwyf was used for quarterly ceremonies marking the solar solstices and equinoxes, for pagan ceremonies of baptism and marriage, as well as for Eisteddfodau held under the auspices of the Gorsedd.

The Rocking Stone itself is one of a number of naturally-occuring glacial boulders scattered along this rocky platform high above the Taff, and lies where it was left by a receding glacier at the end of the last ice age. The complex of stone circles around it were put in place by Archdruid Myfyr Morgannwg in 1849 and consist of an inner ring of twelve standing stones and an outer ring of 28. From the circles, two avenues of stones extend in opposite directions, one of which leads to another circle representing a serpent's head complete with 'eyes' decorated with concentric circles and letters of the bardic alphabet. The whole was designed to represent a serpent swallowing an egg – two key symbols of the neo-Druidic religion.

The Rocking Stone's significance to the neo-Druids derived from the belief that it would have been used by the ancient Celtic druids of pre-Roman and pre-Christian Britain for their own ceremonies. While there is no historical proof to this end, the existence of a Bronze Age funerary ring cairn further along the common to the north certainly suggests that this location had a cermonial significance for the ancient Britons.

Walk Directions: (-) denotes Point of Interest
Standing outside Pontypridd Museum, turn left to cross the old bridge (1). Continue past the Maltsters public house on the opposite side of the road, and cross the road at the crossing to enter Ynysangharad Park. At the fork of paths, take the right hand one that broadly follows the river bank and continue along it around the perimeter of the park. Where it joins a cycle path next to the cricket pitch, turn right along it. Pass under the concrete road bridge before climbing gradually away from the river to a footbridge over the A470 dual carriageway.

Having crossed the footbridge, cross the road and climb the steps to the left of the terraced houses. From the top of the steps, a 200 meter detour to the right brings you to Dr Price's Roundhouses (2). The main route, however, goes left and uphill. You soon come to a turning on the right for Craig yr Helfa Cottages which you should take. Continue until you are almost at the farmyard, where another path heads off to the left to bring you to a kissing-gate next to a finger post. Pass through the gate, and turn right to pick up the broad track (possibly muddy at first) that heads uphill through the woods, through another kissing-gate, and then over a stile. The path continues through a mix of trees, gorse and bracken, through two more kissing-gates, and finally over a stream, to come to a single track road at Hendre Prosser: a longhouse dating back to the 17th century whose circular pigsty is on display at St Fagan's Museum of Welsh Life.

Cross the stile opposite and follow the track over another stile and then through a gate. The path then follows the fence on the left as indicated by the fingerpost (which is actually on the other side of the fence from the path), before crossing a stream and passing through a kissing-gate. Cross the field ahead, passing just to the right of the stone ruins (marked as Tir Cae-mawr on the OS map), and pass through two sets of gateposts to come to a stile next to Ffynnon Rhingyll farm.

Cross the farm track and go over the stile opposite. Follow the fence on your left until you come to a field corner where two stiles – the second of which is fingerposted – bring you to another field.

Cross this field to come to a metal stile (ignore the metal gates either side of it). The path continues through woods, dropping down gradually to a stream before crossing it and passing through a kissing-gate. Once through the gate, turn left to follow first the stream and then a fence around the edge of a marshy field to another stile. Cross the stile and head across the field to another stile which brings you to the mountain road next to Eglwysilan church (3).

Having looked around the church and yard, turn left out of the church gate and retrace your steps back to the stile, then continue past it along the mountain road. At the crossroads, continue straight ahead – waymarked Heritage Trail / Rhymney Ridgeway. After about 800 meters, you come to a gate onto Eglwysilan Common. Enter the common and take

Follow waymark to kissing-gate in wall

the right-hand track at the fork. Continue around the edge of the common for about ¾ of a mile, until you come to a waymark (Heritage Trail) and a kissing-gate in the stone wall on your right. Pass through the gate and follow the line of the grassy track downhill. Continue to follow it until it joins a surfaced track above Parc Mawr farm. Turn left along the track to zigzag past the farm and come to the back of terraced houses in Senghenydd (4).

Turn right and continue along the alley behind the houses until you come to the end of the third and final terrace – Station Road. Follow the road over bridge, then turn right by the old county police station. You soon come to the Aber Heritage Centre on your right. You then need to turn left at the clock, and continue up the main road through Senghenydd to arrive some 400 meters later at the Miners Memorials on your left.

Exiting the Memorials' enclosure, turn left to continue along the same road for a short distance, before turning right at the bus stop. Cross the bridge, and climb uphill past the ends of four terraces, and then along a track past some allotments. Cross a stile

Keep right at fork near farm

as you continue towards Glawnant farm. Just before you reach the farmyard, another track forks off to the right from the main one. Follow this track across a stream and then, as it continues to meander uphill, to come again to the common via a metal gate in a stone wall.

Take red gravel path ahead

Here there are two parallel tracks. Turn left along the higher of the two and follow it until it brings you to a mountain road. Continue along the road in the same direction until it turns sharply left; here, take the path of reddish brown gravel straight ahead.

Continue along the track, ignoring any minor paths leading off it. After about 500 meters the track swings left to join a stone wall. Some 300 meters later, the track forks again, and you should take the right-hand fork heading uphill and away from the wall. From here the return to Pontypridd is straightforward. Continue along this track as it contours around Cefn Eglwysilan, giving breathtaking views of the Taff and Cynon valleys below. (If you want to take in the top of Cefn Eglwysilan, turn left off the track and continue past the masts to the trig point – about 1.5 miles / 2 km there and back.) Eventually the track gradually loses height and joins a metalled road. Turn right along the road which brings you downhill to the outskirts of Pontypridd. At the junction with a red post box, turn left along the road then take the path on the right soon after onto the common.

You will soon see the stone circle (5) ahead of you, providing another viewpoint over Pontypridd. At this point, turn right to pass the war memorial and then, having taken the left option at the fork, down some steps to the road. Cross the road and take another road straight ahead past Llanover House to come to a large roundabout. Use the pedestrian crossings to pass under the fly-over, then past the Llanover Arms to come back to your start point next to the old bridge.

Abertillery – Blaenavon

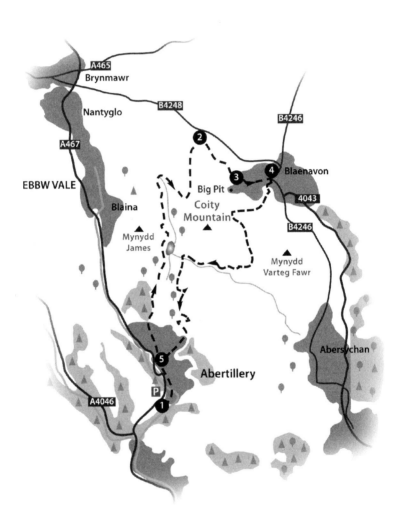

6. Abertillery – Blaenavon

Approx distance: 14.5 miles / 23 km

Approx time: 7.5 hours

O.S Maps: 1: 50,000 OS Landranger Sheets 161 & 171
1: 25,000 OS Explorer Sheets 152 & OL13
(recommended)

Start & End: Car park opposite Tŷ Ebbw Fach, Six Bells, nr Abertillery. Post code: NP13 2ND

Access: From the A467 between Aberbeeg and Abertillery, follow the signs for Six Bells and The Guardian. The turning is on the right if you're heading northwards towards Abertillery, and the car park is on the right after you cross a bridge over the Ebbw Fach.

Parking: As above.

Terrain: A mixture of open country, tracks, paths, and roadside walking, with a couple of potentially boggy sections. Some navigation skills may be needed on the mountain sections in bad visibility.

Please note: At 14.5 miles long and with around 650 meters / 2,145 feet ascent, this is certainly the longest, and quite probably the most strenuous, of the walks in this book. Even on the longest of summer days, the limitations of opening hours mean it would be difficult to complete the full walk and do proper justice to all the attractions en route in one go. Fortunately, the shape of the route makes it easy to adapt into two shorter walks.

A 10 mile walk taking in the Guardian, Abertillery and the upper Tyleri valley is possible by following the main route from Tŷ Ebbw Fach to the point on Coety Mountain where the main route turns left

towards Blaenavon. At this point you can carry on
for around 200 meters to come to a track that
turns off to the right, which will lead you back
down into the valley to re-join the main route at
Gwrhyd farm.

Another 10 mile route taking in the upper Tyleri
valley, Blaenavon and the hills in between, would
start from Cwmtillery village – you can park next
to the lower lake. The green metal barrier and the
path that climbs towards a culvert on the main
route is only 200 meters along the road to the west
of the lake. On the return leg, don't turn left onto
the path after Gwrhyd farm, but continue along
the road to return to your start point.

Facilities: *Tŷ Ebbw Fach at the start point has a cafe and*
toilets, as does the Abertillery & District Museum,
and Big Pit, Ironworks and Heritage Centre at
Blaenavon.

Points of Interest

1. Parc Arael Griffin and the 'Guardian of the Valleys'

Parc Arael Griffin is a local nature reserve on the banks of the Ebbw Fach (*Ebwy Fach*) river occupying the former site of the Six Bells Colliery, just south of the village of the same name.

Arael Griffin was the name of the original colliery sunk in 1863. After a period of disuse in the 1880s, two 330 metre deep shafts were sunk in the mid 1890s. The new mine was worked for the first time in 1889, and closed finally just one year short of a century later in 1988.

On 18 June 1960, Six Bells Colliery was the site of one of the

The Guardian of the Valleys

most recent major mining disasters in Wales when 45 men were killed by an underground explosion caused by a spark from a stone falling onto an iron girder. To mark the 50th anniversary of the disaster in 2010, the 20 metre high sculpture of a miner was erected on the site as a memorial. Designed and created by artist Sebastien Boyesen, it comprises 20,000 strips of steel welded together, and stands on a massive sandstone plinth containing the names of those who died in the disaster.

2. Pontypool and Blaenavon Railway

The Pontypool and Blaenavon Railway is a heritage railway that runs between the Whistle Halt at its northern end and Blaenavon (*Blaenafon*) town. The Whistle Halt is the highest preserved standard-gauge railway station in Britain, and at this end the track is the steepest in Britain. The train runs on weekends during spring and summer.

The 2 mile stretch is all that remains of a railway that once extended from Pontypool (*Pontypŵl*) to Brynmawr. Opened in 1866, the railway originally carried coal from the collieries around Blaenavon to the Heads of the Valleys railway line at Brynmawr, from where it was transported to the English Midlands. The extention of the line southwards to Abersychan and Pontypool in

1880 established a rail link between Blaenavon and the docks at Newport.

The line to Pontypool remained operational carrying coal until Big Pit closed in 1980, after which the track was lifted, leaving only a mile-long section which was re-opened as a tourist attraction in 1983. The line was extended to Blaenavon High Level station in 2010, and to Big Pit in 2011.

The Whistle Inn at the northern end of the railway makes an appealing place for a refreshment stop, not least because of its interesting collection of miners' lamps.

3. Big Pit (Pwll Mawr)

Situated on a bleak hillside above Blaenavon, the award-winning Big Pit Museum was initially opened by a charitable trust in 1983, just three years after it closed as a coal mine. It become part of the National Museums and Galleries of Wales in 1999 – a year before the whole of Blaenavon was designated a UNESCO World Heritage Site – and was extensively revamped before being re-opened in 2004.

The museum includes audio-visual displays and exhibitions, but it is the range of original colliery buildings and features that makes it a unique attraction for anyone interested in the history of coal mining, including a blacksmith's forge, stables, miners' canteen, explosives magazine, winding house, pithead baths and locker room. The highlight for many will be the underground tour, descending the 90 metre shaft guided by former miners able to share their own personal experiences working underground.

Coal had been mined in various pits on this site since the 1820s, but Big Pit itself dates to the sinking of a shaft in 1860 that gained its name from its unusually large size, being the first shaft in Wales able to take two tramways. For the next 120 years, it was the most important pit in Blaenavon, employing nearly 1,400 men at its peak in 1923. Production and employment gradually declined in the second half of the 20th century, and the pit was closed in 1980.

4. Blaenavon Ironworks

This CADW owned site is the jewel in the crown of the Blaenavon World Heritage Site and is a rarity for CADW sites in that entry is free.

Established by three businessmen from the English Midlands in 1789 in an area then known as 'Lord Abergavenny's Hills', the ironworks were one of the most important in the world over the period that followed, when the need for weaponry to fight the Napoleonic Wars and the expansion of the railways meant that the demand for iron was high. Men arrived from all over Wales, the west of England, and Ireland to take up work, many of them living in company-owned housing such as Stack Square and Engine Row which can still be seen on the site.

In the 1860s, steel started to be produced at nearby Forgeside, thanks in part to new techniques that had been developed at the Blaenavon works. The conversion to steel, however, was the beginning of a period of decline for the original ironworks as iron production fell, with the company increasingly focussed on steel and coal. Production ceased completely in 1904.

Work to preserve the site started in 1974, and today the Blaenavon Ironworks are considered to be the best-preserved example of their kind and age in Britain. As well as the workers' cottages, visitors can view the remains of the blast furnaces, cast houses, a restored water balance tower, and a re-built company shop.

About 300 meters from the Ironworks site is the Blaenavon World Heritage Centre in the old St Peter's School building. The centre provides an overview of the Blaenavon World Heritage Site, and includes exhibitions, displays, a gallery and shop.

Blaenavon Ironworks

Cwm Tyleri and its Reservoir

5. Abertillery (Abertyleri)

Abertillery takes its name from its position at the confluence of the Tyleri and Ebbw Fach rivers, and occupies a quite spectacular position surrounded by steep hillsides in all directions. Unlike the more northern reaches of the two Ebbw valleys around Ebbw Vale and Nantyglo, this area was not reached by the first wave of industrialisation in the 18th century, allowing a traveller in 1799 to remark on 'an extensive district well peopled, richly wooded, and highly cultivated, almost rivalling the fertile counties of England.... we looked down with delight upon numerous valleys which abound with romantic scenery.'

However, ironmasters from further up the valley soon started surveying the area for coal to supply their works, and the sinking of the Cwmtillery Colliery in 1850 brought the first major indus-trialisation to the area. Still, it wasn't until the turn of the 20th century that Abertillery experienced the major population boom (from 6,000 in 1881 to 40,000 in 1921) that saw it become the second-largest town in Monmouthshire after Newport. Much of the town's surviving historical architecture dates from this period, as does Cwmtillery Reservoir at the head of the valley.

The Abertillery & District Museum has an impressive range of exhibits on display charting the area's history from the Stone Age to the present day. Check the museum's website *www.abertilleryand districtmuseum.org.uk* for more information and opening times.

Walk directions

Pass through the gate at the far end of the car park, and follow the path through Parc Arael Griffin until you come to the Guardian of the Valleys (1). From the monument, retrace your steps towards the car park. Just before the gate, turn right and then left through a barrier, and right again to join a cycle path, and then left along the cycle path itself.

The path passes through woods and past a waterworks site, before eventually joining Castle Street in Abertillery (*Abertyleri*). Turn left along the street and continue along it, past the supermarket on your left, until you come to a zebra crossing in front of the library. Cross the road, then continue in the same direction, before turning right immediately after the fire station. Continue uphill until the first junction, where you should turn left up Gladstone Street, next to the Doll's House bar. At the blue 'one way' signs some 100 meters later, turn right up Portland Street. Follow this street straight ahead, as it changes names. Keep right at the fork with a red phone box, to continue climbing up Tŷ Bryn Hill, until eventually you leave the houses behind and the street becomes a wooded lane, levelling out as it does so. After about 500 meters, you come to some more houses – turn right and downhill at the fork. Some 250 meters later, a track heads off uphill to the left, through a green metal barrier.

Follow this track until it crosses a culvert, at which point you should take the grassy path which heads off to the right *before* the culvert. Follow this path past some old quarry remains and through a large metal gate, and then along the hillside above Cwmtillery Reservoir, until after about ¾ mile you come to the hollow of Pant Du. The path curves around the edge of the hollow, following a dry stone wall on the right. About half way around, opposite a gap in the wall, another path heads off half-left and uphill.

In summer, the path may be obscured in parts by bracken. It climbs gradually up the steep valley side before following the edge of the plateau at the top. Eventually, the path descends slightly to a marshy dip that is the source of the Tyleri river. Cross the headstream and climb again on the other side until you come to a fenced-off enclosure. Turn right and then left around the enclosure to come to an unsurfaced mountain track. Turn right along the track, which is soon joined by a wall to your right.

After about ½ mile, and opposite a large metal gate in the wall, another path heads off to the left, which you should take. Keep left at the fork soon after to follow this track to the saddle between Cefn Coch and Twyn Ffynhonnau Goerion, and then downhill towards Blaenavon (*Blaenafon*).

Stay on the same path as it crosses a metalled track, then cross a stile before passing through a gate. Turn left along the surfaced track and continue past the Whistle Inn on your right (2). After crossing the bridge, turn right down a cycle path, keeping right so that the ponds are on your left. Keep right again at the next two junctions of paths and again at a third junction after crossing a wooden footbridge. Pass through a small wooden gate, and turn right down the road, then left soon after down another cycle path. Follow the cycle path as signposted, including across a road between the Rhymney Brewery and Big Pit (3). Soon after crossing the road, another path forks off to the left through a kissing-gate, signposted Heritage Town etc. Take this path and follow it through woods then past reed beds until you come, via two metal gates, to the road. Turn left here and follow the signs for Blaenavon Ironworks (4) about 300 meters away, and then return to this point.

The main route continues right from the gate, and downhill – signposted Big Pit. Follow the road across a stream and then sharply uphill, keeping right at the fork to continue along Forgeside Road. Continue over the railway bridge to a junction. The route continues straight ahead along a gravelly track through the gate opposite.

Continue uphill past farm buildings and through two metal gates until the track swings left – at this point leave it and take the path through a gate to the right, indicated by a footpath waymark.

Take path through gate on right

This section can be wet and boggy in parts: the driest ground is usually found close to the fence on your right. After about 400 meters you come to a stone ruin, where you should bear left as indicated by the waymark. Follow a sheepwalk through the rushes, climbing gradually towards the track that can be seen clearly contouring the hillside ahead.

At the point where you meet the track, another path heads uphill opposite. Take this path and follow it for a mile as it initially climbs and then very gradually loses height. Keep right at the fork as

indicated by a waymark sign, to drop down to a stream. Cross the stream and follow the track as it broadly follows the line of a stone wall for another half a mile. It becomes stony and crosses another stream before climbing the opposite bank.

Keep right at fork

At the brow of the hill, pass the white gas pipe-line marker on your left to come to a crossroads of tracks, where you should continue straight ahead. The track now drops gradually for about a mile, to join a single track road at the bottom.

Turn left along the road and then, just as you pass Gwrhyd farm, turn half-left onto a path which cimbs away from the road – take the lower and most distinct of the two tracks on offer. Follow this track as it contours along the valley side for over a mile, until it brings you to a large metal gate next to a cattle grid in a corner. Pass through the gate and turn right, downhill, keeping left at the fork to come to a stone building and ruins (shown as Greenmeadow on the OS map). Do a hairpin turn around the building to continue your descent on a surfaced track which brings you, via another metal gate, to the upper part of Abertillery.

Keep left at the fork next to the grit bin, and continue downhill until you come to a crossroads with Heolgerrig and High Street. Turn right down High Street and then, some 150 meters later, left down Market Street opposite the multi-storey car park. Here you will find Abertillery and District Museum (5) on the left. Continue to the end of Market Street, then turn right down King Street. At the bottom of King Street, you are back on Castle Street where you were earlier on in the walk.

Turn left along Castle Street and then, having passed the large junction for the supermarket, right onto the cycle path to retrace your steps back to the start point.

Ebbw Vale – Pontlottyn

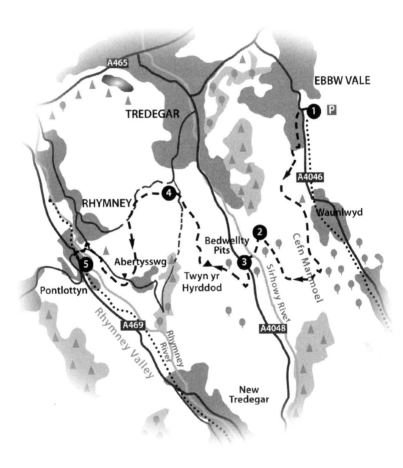

7. Ebbw Vale – Pontlottyn

Approx distance: 10 miles / 15 km

Approx time: 5 hours

O.S Maps: 1: 50,000 OS Landranger Sheet 171

1: 25,000 OS Explorer Sheet 166 (recommended)

Start: The walk starts at Ebbw Vale Town railway station and ends at Pontlottyn railway station. Both stations have regular trains to Cardiff, about an hour's journey away from each. It takes about 1 hour 20 minutes to return from Pontlottyn to Ebbw Vale by bus. Plan your journey at www.traveline-cymru.info.

Access: Ebbw Vale Town rail station is in the centre of Ebbw Vale town, on the Works site. Pontlottyn is just south of Rhymney, on the A460 Rhymney to Caerphilly road. Both stations are signposted.

Parking: There is parking at Ebbw Vale Town railway station.

Terrain: Mostly clear paths and tracks, with some cross country sections on Cefn Manmoel, Mynydd Bedwellty and around Cefn Golau. There are some roadside sections, particularly at the start and end of the walk.

Please note: The walk has a moderate total ascent and descent of 350m / 1,155 feet. The walk has an 'm' shape, involving climbs at the start and mid-way points with some flatter walking and descents inbetween and at the end. Route finding on Mynydd Bedwellty could be tricky in poor visibility.

Facilities: Pontlottyn has the facilities typical of a good-sized village, including convenience stores and public houses. Ebbw Vale, being a large town, even more so.

Points of Interest

1. Ebbw Vale

Ebbw Vale (*Glynebwy*) was one of the first parts of the valleys to be industrialised, and one of the last to lose its heavy industry. It lies at the heart of the heads of the valleys region, stretching from Hirwaun to Blaenavon, which saw numerous ironworks established in the late 18th century, when the plentiful local supply of iron ore along with accessible coal and limestone made the area an ideal location for the new coke-fired furnaces. The first furnace in the valley was erected at Beaufort in 1778, and the first in Ebbw Vale istelf in 1790.

During the 19th century, Ebbw Vale was at the forefront of innovation in the steel industry, with the world's first ever steel rail being forged in the town in 1857. After experiencing a slump in the late 19th and early 20th centuries, the works were completely rebuilt in 1936, and by the 1940s had become the largest steelworks in Europe. Steel continued to be produced in the town until 1978 when British Steel closed the works at the cost of 4,500 jobs. Tinplate working continued until 2001, when it too came to an end and the works closed. Redevelopment of the massive 200 acre site started in 2002; Ebbw Vale Parkway railway station and Aneurin Bevan Hospital were among the first new developments, with the site also being used to host the National Eisteddfod of Wales in 2010.

Ebbw Vale

Fountain Inn, Troedrhiwgwair

While iron and steel were the first and last of the heavy industries in the area, Ebbw Vale was also a major coal mining centre. Coal was mined for use in the ironworks from the start, but from the 1870s the Ebbw Vale Steel, Iron & Coal Company – which by virtue of the quantities needed to fuel the works was already the largest coal producer in south Wales – switched its focus to producing coal for export, which was shipped around the world from the docks at Newport.

2. Troedrhiwgwair

Troedrhiwgwair was once a thriving village of around a hundred houses, with a school, pub, post office, church and chapel. Like other villages in the area, it developed originally in the late 19th century to house local iron and coal workers. Today, however, only a dozen or so houses remain, dotted along the old main street. In

Sirhywi valley from above Bedwellty Pits

1973, a report commissioned by the local council in the wake of the Aberfan disaster advised that there was a danger of a landslide from the hill above. Over subsequent years, most of the houses and other buildings were demolished, though the fears of disaster have so far proved unfounded.

If you stand where the footpath joins the road, on your right are the remains of the village school, while slightly higher up the hillside stood the ominously-named Armageddon Chapel. The Fountain Inn on your left was, as its appearance suggests, originally a farm. Used as an inn from the 1860s onwards, one of its unusual features was a meeting room for the Royal & Ancient Order of Buffaloes. Having changed little in the intervening century and a half, the pub closed its doors in the early 2000s, shortly after the death of the last landlady Marge Mason – the pub having been known locally for many years as 'Marge's Farm'.

3. Bedwellty Pits

There can be no doubt about the origin of this village, though the eponomous pit, which stood to the north of the houses and which was operational from 1850–1939, has long disappeared. Sunk by the Tredegar Iron and Coal Company, it produced steam coal and ironstone and at its peak employed almost 1,200 men.

While the pit is gone, it has left its mark in the form of the landscaped coal waste that lies between the village and the Sirhywi river, and on the hillside to the west. On the same hillside, at the head of a disused tramway on the edge of a former quarry, stands the winding gear of a self-acting haulage engine which was used to lower stone from the quarry to the village below. As well as providing a solitary reminder of the industry that once dominated here, the spot also provides spectacular views of the Sirhowy valley.

4. Cefn Golau Cholera Cemetery

This cemetery must be one of the most haunting sites in south Wales. As the town of Tredegar sprang up quickly around the ironworks in the early 19th century, living conditions were cramped and squalid, facilitating the spread of disease.

There were three major cholera outbreaks in Tredegar, in 1832, 1849 and 1866. Fear of the disease known as the 'King of Terror' meant that victims were not allowed to be buried in the town cemeteries and were brought instead to this bleak spot on the mountainside. In fact, such was the fear and shame associated with the disease that many families buried their dead at night, and it was often difficult to find enough people to help with the burial.

It is estimated that over two hundred people are buried in this small plot, though only twenty-six complete gravestones remain. They span all three outbreaks, though the majority come from 1849, and have a mixture of Welsh and English inscriptions.

5. Blast Furnace Inn and Viaduct

The Blast Furnace Inn was opened in 1845 by a Mr Jenkin Edwards, who was at that time manager of the Bute and Rhymney Iron Furnace, and converted his manager's house into an inn.

Nearby stands Pontlottyn's most impressive landmark – the viaduct. Constructed from 1850 onwards using local stone, it comprises of ten arches and continues to carry the railway which links Rhymney with Cardiff. In 1867, a Mrs Williams built the Railway Inn under two of the viaduct's arches on land rented from the Railway Company, much to the displeasure of the Rhymney Iron Company which had refused permission for her to build an inn on their land for fear of affecting their workers' efficiency. The inn – which consisted of two separate buildings, one under each arch – stood until 1997, when the railway company sadly forced its removal for maintenance purposes.

Walk Directions: (-) denotes Point of Interest

Exit the railway station, and take the Ebbw Vale (1) Mechanical Link to bring you up to a main road. Turn left along the road, then cross it to take the first right onto The Walk. Continue straight ahead at the mini roundabout, then follow the road as it swings left and continues to climb gradually. Continue along this street, until you come to the large Christ Church with its tower on your left. Here you need to turn right up Spencer Street, which heads sharply uphill opposite the church.

Continue to climb along the same road, now bearing the name Commercial Street, and follow it as it does a 'hairpin turn' to the right. Go up the steps next to the RTB Rugby Club, and turn left up High Street, continuing until it ends at a gate leading to a rough track.

Pass through the gate and follow the track as it climbs gradually up the open hillside. After about ½ mile, just before you pass under some power lines, there is a crossroads in the track. Turn left at the crossroads to follow a track that contours to the left of, and below, the highest part of the ridge ahead. At the fork after the wooden gatepost, keep left to drop down to the left of the quarry before climbing back up to rejoin the other track next to an old engine house.

Continue along the clear track ahead, as indicated by the footpath sign until, around ¾ mile later, you come to a small cliff face where another path heads off sharply right. Take this path and follow it across the top of Mynydd Manmoel until you come to a single track road.

In front of you, there is an enclosed field with tracks for motorcycles laid out in it. You need to pass to the right-hand side of this field, keeping close to its perimeter fence. Eventually you come to a corner of the field, and the fence heads off away from you to the left. At this point, follow the grassy track straight ahead and downhill towards a woodland, with the Sirhywi river in the valley below you to your left. The path becomes more distinct as you head into the woods, and continues through them until you come to a stile next to some huts. Cross the stile, and you come out onto a metalled track at Troedrhiwgwair (2).

Turn left past the deserted Fountain Inn and follow the footpath sign through a kissing-gate and onwards along a stream to a footbridge over the Sirhywi river and on to the houses of Bedwellty Pits (3). Pass through a kissing-gate and head uphill to come to a main road. Turn left along the main road: take care as this can be quite a busy road – it is best to stay on the left side until the bend, and then cross to the right side. After about 300 meters, you pass a ruined school building on the right and soon after there is a large metal gate. Go through the gate, and head across the field away from the road until you come to a concrete track. Turn right and head uphill.

Turn left off the main track and cross the stream that runs through the dark gravel to head up the grassy slope towards the overgrown tips ahead. By bearing right as you approach the first mound, then skirting around it, you will come to the old winding gear (3). From here, take the path that zig-zags around the tip on the left to join a grassy track that follows the line of a fence for a short distance, before bearing left away from it. Continue through the gate and follow the track until it peters out at the corner of the fence and stone wall. From here, head directly uphill in a westerly direction across open country towards the highest point on the horizon ahead, to come to the trig point at Twyn yr Hyddod.

From Twyn yr Hyddod, turn right to follow the track along the

ridge northwards to the cairn at Carn Stwpa, and from there drop down towards the pond you can see ahead of you to the left. Cross the road and follow the path to the left of the pond to come to Cefn Golau Cholera Cemetery (4).

The cairn at Carn Stwpa

From the cemetery, continue to follow the edge of the pond to its far end. From here, you need to pick a route through the rushes towards the farm buildings to the west, aiming for just to the right of the whitewashed farmhouse, where a footbridge crosses a narrow stream. From the bridge, you head up the bank to come to the main road via the farm track. Turn left along the road until you come to the entrance for Tredegar and Rhymney Golf Club.

Head towards the clubhouse, and through the small metal gate in the wall to the left. Pass to the left of the clubhouse and past its outbuildings, then follow the line of the fence along the perimeter of the golf course. You climb slowly at first, before starting to descend along the edge of a fairway, keeping close to the fence throughout. Eventually, at the far corner of the course you arrive at a green and tee. Pass to the left of the green and cross the stile behind the no.6 tee.

Continue downhill until you come to the first row of houses in Abertysswg. Turn right along the slightly elevated grassy path between the rushes, until you come to a gate which takes you onto a road. Turn left along the road, then right down the path next to the bus stop. Continue until you get to a cycle path. Turn right along it to head north towards Pontlottyn.

Follow the cycle path until you come to the school, then turn right and uphill, to come to the main road. Turn left along it, and then left again when you come to a junction. Follow the road as it sweeps right, past the Blast Furnace Inn (5) on your left, and under the viaduct. Turn left along Merchant Street and you soon come to the railway station, on the left behind the Empire Club.

Pontlottyn – Troedyrhiw

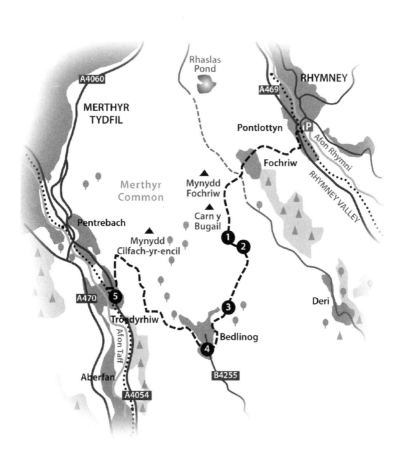

8. Pontlottyn – Troedyrhiw

Approx distance: 8 miles / 12 km

Approx time: 4 hours

O.S Maps: 1: 50,000 OS Landranger Sheet 170 & 171

1: 25,000 OS Explorer Sheet 166 (recommended)

Start & End: The walk starts at Pontlottyn railway station and ends at Troedyrhiw railway station. Both stations have regular trains to Cardiff, about an hour's journey away from each. It also takes about an hour to return from Troedyrhiw to Pontlottyn by bus, changing at Merthyr Tydfil Bus Station. Plan your journey at www.traveline-cymru.info.

Access: Pontlottyn is just south of Rhymney, on the A460 Rhymney to Caerphilly road. Troedyrhiw is just south of Merthyr Tydfil on the A4054, just off the A470 main Cardiff to Merthyr Tydfil road. Both stations are signposted.

Parking: There is parking at Pontlottyn railway station.

Terrain: Mostly clear paths and tracks, but with some cross-country sections – especially over Mynydd Fochriw and Carn y Bugail. Some roadside walking through the villages en route.

Please note: The walk has a moderate total ascent of around 400m / 1,320 feet. The walk is an 'm' shape, involving climbs at the start and mid-way points with some flatter walking and descents inbetween. Route-finding on the cross-country sections around Mynydd Fochriw and Carn y Bugail can be tricky in poor visibility, so please ensure you are properly prepared in such conditions.

Facilities: *Pontlottyn, Fochriw, Bedlinog and Troedyrhiw all have the typical facilities of small and medium sized villages, including convenience stores and public houses. There are no public toilets along the route.*

Points of Interest

1. Carn y Bugail

The two cairns at Carn y Bugail – one underneath the trig point, and another just north of it, both belong to the Bronze Age. They form part of a series of fourteen or so cairns that follow the line of the ridge and which may be associated with an ancient route running along it.

The main cairn is circular, with a diameter of 16 meters and a height of up to three meters. Excavations around the year 1700 found three parallel cists containing urns and burnt bones. Like the other cairns on the mountain, it has been damaged through having some of its stones removed over the years.

Just to the east of Carn y Bugail is the Roman road known as Heol Adam that ran north-south linking the two forts at Gelligaer and Penydarren. You can still make out its path today, as you cross it on your way to Carreg Fain Hir.

2. Carreg Fain Hir Standing Stone

About 2.5 meters high, and standing at a 45 degree angle, this standing stone is shrouded in mystery.

When the stone was first studied in the 17th century, an inscription of eight letters was visible at its base, variously recorded as REFSOIHI, TEFROIHI, TEFROVTI or NEFROIHI. Its style suggested a 6th or 7th century origin, and most likely represented

Carn y Bugail

Carreg Fain Hir

Bedlinog Wetland

Bedlinog

a Romanised personal name. Sadly, the inscription was destroyed in the late 1800s by – so the story goes – a group of drunken miners from Dowlais who took it upon themselves to 'test the quality of the stone'.

The stone stands next to a low horseshoe-shaped bank, which may be older in origin and could mark the site of another Bronze Age cairn or burial mound.

3. Bedlinog Mines

It is hard to imagine that this tranquil and seemingly secluded wetland was once a vast industrial site employing up to 2,000 men and producing over 5,000 tonnes of coal a week.

The Bedlinog Drift mine was situated at the eastern end of the site (to your left) and was driven into the hillside. It operated between 1929 and 1956, linking up underground with another drift mine on the other side of the hill, over a mile to the north.

Bedlinog Colliery was by far the larger of the two enterprises, and was a deep mine sunk into the ground. The site of one shaft is still just about identifiable among the reeds on your left (at grid reference SO 097 016) as you walk towards Bedlinog. Sunk in 1874 by the Dowlais Iron, Coal and Steel Company, production ceased in 1924 as the focus of coal production moved further down the valley towards Treharris. While many of the men gained work in the newer collieries, the resulting unemployment contributed to the social unrest that followed (see walk 3).

4. Bedlinog

Situated on a steep hillside on the eastern side of the Taf Bargoed valley, Bedlinog is in many ways a typical mining village. Its isolated location however, with no other towns or villages in sight and surrounded by steep hillsides, means it has a more rural feel than most.

The area had been well farmed since the Middle Ages, and until the 19th century the upper Taf Bargoed valley comprised of a handful of farms along with a mill near the river at Cwmfelin – the lower part of the modern village. The sinking of the first coal mines in the 1870s brought rapid growth, and a population of 5,000 by 1914.

In the 1930s, Bedlinog gained a reputation as a hot-bed of radicalism and social unrest (see walk 3). Nicknamed 'Little Moscow', the Communist Party had a strong following in the village (including a Communist Drama Society and a Communist Chamber of Commerce) and Bedlinog contributed more than its share of volunteers for the International Brigade of the Spanish Civil War.

A plaque at 29 Commercial Street commemorates the Rev. Gwilym Davies, who was the founder of the 'Peace Message of the Children of Wales' first sent in 1922 and still done so annually by Urdd Gobaith Cymru. The Rev. Davies was also a major influence in the founding of UNESCO.

More recently, Bedlinog was the location for the filming of the pilot episode of 'Porridge'. Fans of the series will remember the scene where Fletcher sabotages a prison van by relieving himself in the fuel tank. It was filmed on Graig Road in Bedlinog.

5. Saron Cemetery

In 1835, Saron Congregationalist Chapel was the first to be built in the new village of Troedyrhiw, and it was expanded in 1852 to include the graveyard. An imposing building, overlooking the village from its position on the hillside, the chapel was a prominent village landmark until it was demolished in 1990.

The cemetery, which includes burials from the 1830s to the 1980s, has remained as a reminder of this former religious and cultural centre. Until recently it was overgrown and derelict, but a local group is now working to secure the future of this historic site.

Walk Directions: (-) denotes Point of Interest
Turn right out of Pontlottyn station then left at the Empire Club, and then left again along the main road. Take the right turn signposted Fochriw and follow this road around, past Pontlottyn Primary School, until you come to Fochriw Road. Just after the last house on the left side of Fochriw Road, a footpath passes through a kissing-gate onto the hillside. Take this path, and then head directly uphill until you come to another kissing-gate at the top.

Pass through the gate and turn right, following the fence until you come to a single track road. Cross the road and pick a path through the rushes towards the houses you can see ahead of you to the right. As you approach the houses, bear left to come to a stile that leads to a path between two fences. Turn left along this path to come to the main road through Fochriw via a gate next to the football pitch. Turn left along the main road, and follow it through, and then out of, the village until you come to a cattle grid at the top of the hill.

From the cattle grid, Mynydd Fochriw rises before you to the right. Leave the road and head cross country and directly uphill, aiming initially for the old workings that you can see on the hillside above. Cross a road to come to the workings, and then head up the grassy track until it

Head through rushes towards the houses

111

peters out, at which point you should continue to head uphill cross country. By continuing to head away from Fochriw in a generally south-westerly direction, and aiming always for the highest point ahead, you will soon come to the flatter terrain of the summit plateau of Mynydd Fochriw.

By now, Carn y Bugail (1) will dominate the horizon to the south of you. It looks rather imposing from this angle, but the climb is actually short and gentle. Head directly towards it, until you reach the cairns and trig point at its summit.

The Carreg Fain Hir standing stone (2) is found to the east-south-east of the summit. To find it, stand at the trig point and turn so that your back is towards the opencast mine and head off in the direction you are facing, which should be about 45° to the left of the obvious track that heads off the summit. Very soon, you will see the standing stone ahead of you.

From the stone, turn right along the broad grassy track that runs next to it and head southwards until you come to a mountain road next to some boulders. Cross the road and turn right along it to come to a footpath fingerpost. Take the general direction indicated by the fingerpost, but bear slightly right (west) using the quarry on the opposite hillside as a target, so that you descend very soon into a marshy dip where a stone ruin (shown as 'Pen-marc' on the OS Explorer map) stands next to a line of half a dozen trees. Cross the stile next to the ruin, and head directly across the field to the stile opposite. Repeat for the next three stiles and fields, until you come to a gate next to a stream. Pass through the gate and follow the stream on your left to come to a kissing-gate leading onto a road.

Turn right along the road and very soon take the signed footpath through the kissing-gate on your left. Follow the path along the left bank of the stream until it crosses the stream and descends into a wetland clearing (3). The path now becomes more distinct, and you should continue to follow it, staying on the right bank of the Nant Llwynog stream (do not cross the footbridge).

You soon come to a tarmac road near a red brick hut and, after passing the children's playground, turn left to pass in front of the first row of houses and follow the track over a small bridge and then uphill past a cattle grid. Where the track then bends left, pass through the gate in front of you and follow the path gradually downhill, with the Nant Llwynog stream now below you on your right. Pass through the kissing-gate and over the bridge over the railway, then turn right along the metalled road to continue downhill and emerge at Bedlinog village (4) square next to the rugby club.

Pass the war memorial and turn right onto Commercial Street. Continue along this street. For a while you leave the houses (and pavement) behind, but soon come to another row of houses – Hylton Terrace. Just before the mini roundabout, take the path on the left, next to the convenience store, and head down to

Pass through gate in front of you

the footbridge. Cross the bridge and, at a crossroads of paths, take the one straight ahead, climbing quite steeply uphill until you come to the edge of a farmyard at the top.

Pass straight ahead at crossroads

Turn right and take the sheep's track that follows the fence along the hillside – take care not to take the more distinct grassy track that heads back downhill. Eventually the path passes through a ruined dry stone wall onto the common. Turning your back to the valley below, head westwards across the rough grassland. Cross the mountain road, and continue straight ahead until you come to a fence running north-south (if you first encounter a stone wall, pass through one of the many gaps in it and continue to the fence).

Turn right at the fence and follow it northwards for some time, until you come to the remains of a small quarry next to a stream. Cross the stream and then the stile next to it. Here the fence forks, one going uphill and the other downwards. Between them is a grassy path which is generally flat and straight for about 400 meters, before it swings leftwards and heads sharply downhill. Take care, as this section can be muddy and wet.

Continue to follow the path downhill, crossing another path running perpendicular to it, and then passing another much larger old quarry on your left. Soon after, the path forks, and you should take the left-hand option. Do the same again

A grassy path between the fences

soon after, taking the broad track to the left, rather than the narrow path heading downhill to the right. This path eventually joins a cycle path: turn left along it, and then right where it too forks. Cross the street and take the path to the left of the cemetery (5). Turn right along Industrial Terrace then left down Bridge Street to come to Troedyrhiw train station.

Troedyrhiw – Aberdare

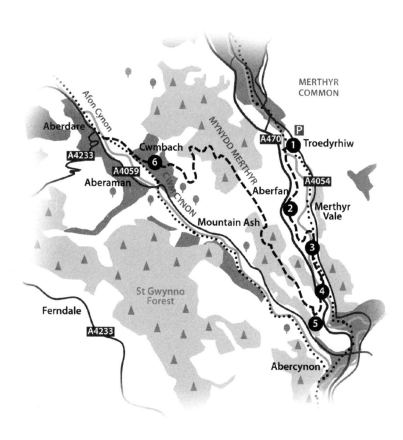

9. Troedyrhiw – Aberdare

Approx distance: 13 miles / 21 km (14 miles with detour to Glamorganshire Canal)

Approx time: 5.5 hours

O.S Maps: 1: 50,000 OS Landranger Sheet 170
1: 25,000 OS Explorer Sheet 166 (recommended)

Start & End: The walk starts at Troedyrhiw railway station and ends at Aberdare railway station. Both stations have regular trains to Cardiff (about an hour's journey away from each) and Pontypridd (about 30 minutes). It also takes about an hour to return from Aberdare to Troedyrhiw by train, changing at Abercynon. Plan your journey at www.traveline-cymru.info.

Access: Troedyrhiw is just south of Merthyr Tydfil on the A4054, just off the A470 main Cardiff to Merthyr Tydfil road. Aberdare lies near the head of the Cynon valley. Both stations are signposted.

Parking: Street parking possible in Troedyrhiw.

Terrain: Mostly clear paths and tracks, with one short cross-country section. Roadside walking towards the end.

Please note: The walk has a moderate total ascent of 500m / 1,650 feet. Terrain is flat to start as you follow the river Taff to Pontygwaith. There is then some steady but not overly strenuous climbing onto the ridge of Cefn y Fan and Mynydd Merthyr, before the gradual descent into Aberdare to finish.

Facilities: Troedyrhiw has all the typical facilities of a village, including convenience stores and public houses, whilst Aberdare is the largest town in the Cynon Valley. The Cynon Valley Museum, and its cafe, just north-west of the railway station is well worth a visit.

Points of Interest

1. Pont Rhun

According to legend, this ancient crossing point over the river Taff (*Taf*) is named for Rhun, son of Brychan Brycheiniog and brother of Saint Tudful, who was killed here in battle in the year 420AD.

The 5th century was a particularly turbulent time in Wales. The Romans had not long left, and foreign raiders were taking advantage of the power vacuum which they left to attack the native Welsh. The story goes that local king Brychan Brycheiniog (who gave his name to the kingdom, and subsequently the county, of Brycheiniog/Brecknock) and his family were visiting one of his children – of which it is said he had somewhere between twenty-four and sixty-three – when they came under attack from a band of Picts and Saxons. Brychan – along with his daughter Tudful and her family – were killed a few miles north of here. It was at that spot that a church was later dedicated to Tudful, from which Merthyr Tydfil (*Merthyr Tudful*) took its name.

Rhun and others escaped southwards, but were pursued by their attackers, and Rhun was himself killed defending the bridge which crossed the Taff at this point. His son Nefydd then gathered the men together and, enraged by the slaughter which they had witnessed, eventually succeeded in driving the invaders away.

In more recent times, Pont Rhun was the site of one of the early charcoal-fuelled ironworks that were established in the area from the 16th century onwards.

2. Aberfan

There is not enough space here to even start to do justice to the tragic history of Aberfan and the suffering and injustice endured by its people. A few bare facts must therefore suffice to inform the passing walker of its story.

Aberfan Garden of Remembrance

Over a period of fifty years, waste from the Merthyr Vale Colliery had been dumped in several tips on the mountainside directly above Aberfan. These tips were made unstable by water emanating from a number of natural springs beneath them.

At 9.15am on Friday 21 October 1966, one of the tips collapsed, sending 150,000 cubic meters of watery debris crashing down the hillside in a wave of slurry 10 meters high. The landslide flattened Hafod Tanglwys Uchaf farm before crossing the canal and railway embankment into the village where it demolished about twenty terraced houses and the greater part of Pantglas Junior School, where children had just sat down for the last day before half term.

A total of 144 lives were lost. 116 of these were children. Subsequent inquiries lay the responsibility for the disaster squarely with the National Coal Board's negligent and indifferent policy towards the safety of the tips.

Penydarren Tramroad

A garden of remembrance now stands on the site of Pantglas Junior School, down some steps to the left of the path as you enter the village. A little further on, the cemetery where most of the victims were buried stands on the hillside to the right. The white marble arches mark the mass grave where many of the children were laid to rest.

3. Penydarren Tramroad

Not long after the completion of the Glamorganshire Canal (see no.5), a dispute arose between Crawshay of Cyfarthfa and the other shareholders, who felt that Crawshay was disproportionately benefiting from it. By 1802, this led to the construction of the Penydarren Tramway along the eastern bank of the Taff to serve the Penydarren, Dowlais and Plymouth ironworks. The tramway transported their produce to the canal at Abercynon (then known as Navigation), thereby by-passing the most congested northern section of the canal.

It was on this tramroad that Richard Trevithick tested the first locomotive steam engine in 1804. Trevithick was working for Samuel Homfray, owner of Penydarren Ironworks, and on 22 February 1804 he successfully completed the 9 mile journey from Penydarren to Abercynon with the engine pulling five wagons, 10 tons of iron, and 70 passangers in just over 4 hours. It is said that the success of the experiment won for Mr Homfray a 1,000 guinea bet with Richard Crawshay of Cyfarthfa. Despite the success of Trevithick's innovation, steam-powered journeys did not become the norm on the tramway for another 25 years.

4. Pontygwaith
Like its namesake in the Rhondda Fach, the bridge is named for its proximity to an early ironworks; a furnace is thought to have been

Pontygwaith

erected on the riverbank here in the 16th century, and to have been destroyed by Cromwellian troops in 1648 on account of the owner's Royalist sympathies. Like Pontrhun to the north, the works were set up by Sussex ironmasters who established themselves in the area in Tudor times, taking advantage of the ready supply of iron ore, flowing water and charcoal from the wooded hillsides.

The bridge itself is one of the oldest surviving over the Taff. It was built in the 18th century, possibly by the architect William Edwards who also built the more famous bridge at Pontypridd.

5. Glamorganshire Canal

The Glamorganshire Canal was built between 1790-94 by the Glamorgan Canal Company. The company was a joint enterprise between local ironmasters who wanted a quicker and more efficient way of getting their products to the docks at Cardiff, than the pack-horses and mules hitherto used. Building a canal in such hilly country wasn't without its challenges, and over the 25 miles between Merthyr and Cardiff the canal dropped a total of 165 meters through a total of fifty locks.

It later carried coal as well as iron, and was also used to carry goods from Cardiff and its docks to supply the towns along its route, but it gradually became obsolete after Merthyr and Cardiff were linked by rail in 1841. Subsidence caused by coal mining also became an increasing problem, and the canal was progressively closed between 1898 and 1951. Today much of the route is taken up by the new A470 road and the Taff Trail cycle path, and only a few short sections remain.

At this site, in addition to the channel and towpath of the canal itself, the stone arch Pont y Dderwen bridge across the canal also remains. Between the canal and the A470 road is the mouth of a disused railway tunnel which passes through the mountain to the

Glamorganshire Canal

Cynon valley on the other side. From 1851 – 1964 the railway which passed through it linked Neath with Pontypool and Newport, and crossed the Taff valley below on one of two adjacent viaducts: the other carrying the Cardiff – Merthyr line.

6. Abernant-y-Groes Colliery
Now surrounded by the houses of Cwmbach, this was the site of the first deep mine sunk in the then rural Cynon valley. A helpful information board provides the history of the colliery.

Walk Directions: (-) denotes Point of Interest
Exiting Troedyrhiw railway station, turn left along Bridge Street and over the Pont Rhun (1) bridge. Having crossed the bridge, turn right and climb slowly uphill until you come to the Taff Trail cycle path near the Dynevor Arms. Turn left along the Taff Trail and head southwards out of Troedyrhiw.

After a mile or so, you come to Aberfan (2), passing the Garden of Remembrance on your left and then the cemetery on your right.

About half a mile after the cemetery, the path crosses a road leading to the houses of Pleasant View on your right. Turn left along this road, and head downhill away from Pleasant View. At the foot of the hill, take the path to the left of Einon Villa and follow it down to the river and over the metal footbridge.

Take the path that passes behind the houses of Crescent Street on the right. You are now on the route of the Penydarren Tramway (3). Within about 200 meters, you pass some old sidings, and a little later a series of stone sleepers are visible. Continue southwards along the path for a little over a mile, between the railway on your left and the river on your right, until you come to a stone arch bridge crossing the path. Take the path heading off to the right to come to the road that crosses the bridge and turn right, away from the bridge.

Path to left of Einon Villa

Pass Pontygwaith Farm (or stop to take in the gardens), and continue over the steep hump of the Pontygwaith (4) bridge, then up the steps to the right, and through the underpass. On the other side of the A470, you come to a point where a number of tracks meet. A left turn provides the option of a detour (about a mile there and back) to view close up the Glamorganshire Canal (5). The main route, however, follows the metalled road that heads uphill straight ahead.

The Glamorganshire Canal is now clearly visible below you on your left. Continue past Cefn Glas Farm and at the cattle grid take the rougher track that heads sharp right through a kissing-gate. Head uphill towards the imposing slope of Craig yr Efail.

When you come to the crest of the ridge, the broad vista of the Cynon valley opens up in front of you. Turn right along the ridge, past the gateposts and stile, and continue along the track as it climbs uphill, following a dry stone wall on your right. The path soon levels out as you regain the crest of the ridge, and passes through a gap in the wall before continuing in the same northward direction with the wall now on your left.

As you approach the woodland ahead, pass back through one of the gaps in the stone wall, and go through the gate that blocks the path to enter the forest. Continue up the stony slope straight ahead, and pass between a trig point and a mast at the summit of Twyn

Pass through gap in stone wall

Clearing above Cynon Valley

Brynbychan. Continue northwards, dropping down to join a forestry track. Turn left along it, then almost immediately turn right to follow the path of the power lines down to another forestry track.

Turn right along this track and continue until you come to a clearing with the Cynon valley visible again to your left. From here, a stony track winds uphill to the right (waymarked Loops & Links), and you should follow this track until you exit the forest again near the top of the hill. At the fork in the track, take the left-hand option which follows the edge of the forest in a northerly direction until you emerge into open country.

Continue straight ahead towards the woods on the horizon ahead. Pass through a gate into the woods and follow the clear path which bears slightly right. You soon emerge into a clearing at a crossroads of paths where you should take the middle option straight ahead (the least distinct of the three options) which climbs gently towards the brow of the hill. After about 500 meters, another track heads off to the left. Turn left along this track and then right at a T-junction of paths soon after. Having climbed very slightly, the path forks, and you should bear left – downhill. Bear left again at a second fork about 200 meters later. Where the track joins another, turn right as signalled by the blue arrow on a marker stone. The track then continues for about 500 meters, before joining yet another at a metal barrier. Turn left and continue gently downhill until you come to a gate on your right leading to a track which is walled on both sides, and which heads downhill past Cefn-Pennar Uchaf farm.

Track heads off to left

At the fork near Plas y Felin take the right-hand option straight ahead towards the TV mast. Continue along the same track as it bears right then left. Pass through green metal gateposts and continue straight ahead and downhill. The track eventually becomes a metalled road as you enter Cwmbach. Continue to descend through the village, turning right along Cwmbach Road at the junction by the Royal Oak. Continue past the site of Abernant-y-Groes colliery (6) with its blue plaque on your left, before arriving at a main road at the bottom of the hill opposite a petrol station.

Turn right along the main road and then, some 100 meters later, left onto the Cynon Trail path. Continue along this canal-side path until you come back to the road. Continue in the same direction along the pavement until you come to Aberdare (*Aberdâr*) railway station and town centre.

Aberdare – Ton Pentre

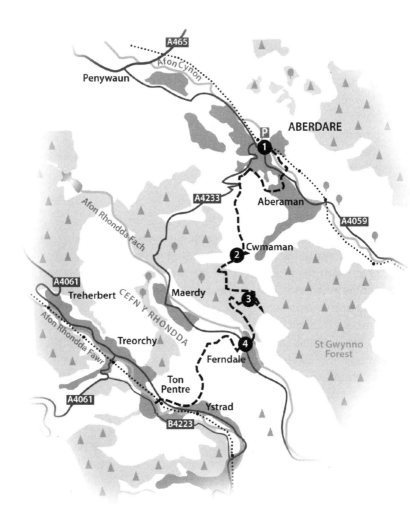

10. Aberdare – Ton Pentre

Approx distance: 11 miles / 17.5 km
Approx time: 5.5 hours
O.S Maps: 1: 50,000 OS Landranger Sheet 170
                    1: 25,000 OS Explorer Sheet 166 (recommended)
Start & End: The walk starts at Aberdare railway station and
                    ends at Ton Pentre railway station. Both stations
                    have regular trains to Cardiff (about an hour's
                    journey away from each) and Pontypridd (about
                    30 minutes). It takes about an hour and 20
                    minutes to return from Ton Pentre to Aberdare by
                    train, changing at Pontypridd. Plan your journey
                    at www.traveline-cymru.info.
Access: Aberdare lies near the head of the Cynon Valley,
                    while Ton Pentre is in the Rhondda Fawr just
                    south-east of Treorchy. Both stations are
                    signposted.
Parking: Parking available at Aberdare station.
Terrain: Mostly clear paths and tracks. Some roadside
                    walking in Aberdare and Ferndale.
Please note: The walk has a total ascent of around 600 meters
                    / 2,000 feet. The terrain is undulating, with
                    alternating climbs and descents as you pass in
                    turn through the Cynon, Aman, Rhondda Fach
                    and Rhondda Fawr valleys.
Facilities: Aberdare is the largest town in the Cynon Valley.
                    The Cynon Valley Museum and its cafe, just north-
                    west of the Railway Station in Aberdare town
                    centre, is well worth a visit. Ferndale and Ton
                    Pentre have convenience stores, public houses
                    and public toilets.

Points of Interest

1. Aberdare

Aberdare (*Aberdâr*) was one of the historic parishes of Glamorgan, and so boasts what is a rarity for the modern valley towns: a medieval parish church. St John's on Green Street dates back to the 12th century. Aberdare remained a small village in a predominantly agricultural area until the turn of the 19th century, when the iron and then coal industries turned it into one of the most vibrant towns in Wales.

Three ironworks were established in the early 1800s, at Llwytgoed and Aber-nant (both 1801) and Gadlys (1827), with the Aberdare Canal opened in 1812 to transport the output to Cardiff and the sea. The coal industry soon established itself in the area too, and it was the primary centre of steam coal production during the middle decades of the 19th century until it was overtaken in that regard by the Rhondda. Iron production in the town ceased during the 1870s; the Gadlys site now houses the Cynon Valley Museum and Gallery, and is well worth a visit.

Much of modern Aberdare's townscape – including chapels, churches and squares – dates from the boom years of the 1850s and 1860s, when such was the pre-eminence of the town as an economic, social and cultural centre that it was said 'what Aberdare thinks today, Wales will think tomorrow'. The first modern National Eisteddfod was held in the town in 1861, and in 1868 Henry Richard, 'the Apostle of Peace', was elected as a Radical Liberal MP for Merthyr Tydfil and Aberdare. The first miner to be elected to Parliament, he became one of the most prominent non-conformists in Westminster, advocating such causes as international peace, disestablishment of the Church and the abolition of slavery.

Aberdare was particularly important as a publishing centre. As well as numerous books and journals, radical newspapers *Y Gwladgarwr* (The Patriot) and *Tarian y Gweithiwr* (The Worker's Shield) were published in the town; the latter being a vocal advocate of the trade union movement and of radical non-conformism. Most of the publishing at that time would have been in Welsh – as late as 1901, over 70% of Aberdare's population were Welsh-speaking.

2. Cwmaman

Today, Cwmaman is probably most famous as the home of the band The Stereophonics, who were formed in the village in 1992. It was also the home of war poet Alun Lewis (1915 – 1944) who was killed while serving in Burma during World War II.

Like much of the valleys, the Aman valley was inhabited only by farmers until the mid-19th century. By the end of the century however, Cwmaman was a thriving village housing the workers of the five pits which surrounded it: Cwmaman, Fforchneol, Cwmneol, Bedwlwyn and Fforchaman. Many of these mines took the names of the nearby farmsteads, and the Fforchaman farm, parts of which date back to the 17th century, still stands – a monument to a bygone age – on the main road next to the Workmen and Social Club. The track that you follow up the hillside opposite once led to Bedwlwyn farmstead; its ruins – including those of a circular pigsty – can still just about be made out among the trees.

In the south-eastern end of the village (about 500 meters along the main road from Fforchaman farm), stands the Cwmaman Workmen's Hall and Institute. Opened in 1892, it is still an impressive building, and typical of the workmen's institutes found throughout valley communities that were paid for the most part by the workers themselves. It once included two halls, a library and reading room, gymnasium, billiards room, band room,

Fforchaman Farm – Cwmaman

and four committee rooms. Unlike many of its contemporaries which are either neglected or demolished (see Ferndale), it is still in use as a community centre, having been renovated on several occasions over the years. While the Institute was the product of the 19th century industrial revolution, behind it stands one of the earliest industrial sites in Glamorgan – the remnants of a 16th century iron furnace.

3. Twyn-y-Briddallt Roman Camp
Of all the ancient tribes of Wales, none resisted the Roman invasion as fiercely as did the Silures in Glamorgan, and it took a series of military campaigns between AD48 and AD79 before the resistance was finally overcome.

The marching camp at Twyn-y-Briddallt bears testament to that period of resistance, and the insecurity of a Roman army on the move in upper Glamorgan at that time. Measuring 402 meters long by 183 wide (roughly the same size as the modern clearing), and protected by a bank and ditch 5.5 meters wide and 1 meter high which would have been topped with a wooden fence, the camp was most likely used only once as a temporary overnight

Twyn-y-Briddallt

base. It is unusual among Roman encampments in that it is of irregular shape, and makes use of the natural prominence of Twyn-y-Briddallt and the steep escarpments on either side of the ridge for added security.

The embankments broadly follow the outline of the clearing, and the fact that the site has been exempted from planting means that the remains have been well preserved. They are at their most distinct along the north-eastern edge of the camp which includes the highest point of Twyn-y-Briddallt, and it is from this point too that the panoramic view that made this such an attractive defensive position can be best appreciated.

4. Ferndale

In 1857, David Davis sunk the first deep coal mine in the Rhondda Fach at Ferndale, eventually extending it to become a complex of nine pits stretching southwards to Tylorstown. Ferndale is

Trerhondda – Ferndale

therefore considered to be the oldest industrial settlement in the Rhondda, a fact reflected in its older name of Trerhondda (Rhondda Town). Walking through the town you will pass examples of buildings typical of valley communities, including chapels of various denominations, a number of working men's clubs, and a rugby club.

Between them, Ferndale and adjoining Blaenllechau boast ten chapel and four church buildings. The impressive Grade 2 listed Trerhondda Welsh Independent Chapel stands right at the heart of Ferndale. Built in 1867 and extended and modified soon afterwards to serve the fast-growing congregation, it is the oldest chapel in the Rhondda Fach. The chapel closed in 1994 and is now used as a community hall. Behind it once stood the Workmen's Hall and Institute, sadly demolished in the mid-1990s. Opened in 1909 at a cost of over £17,000 it was one of the largest of its kind in south Wales, including such amenities as a swimming pool and rifle range in addition to the more usual cinema, library and billiards room.

The walk leaves Ferndale via the Darran Park, a public park built around the natural lake of Llyn y Forwyn which nestles in a hollow below the cliffs of Craig Rhondda Fach – a scar left behind by a landslide at the end of the last ice age. The park was developed in the early 20th century to provide facilities for outdoor recreation and relaxation to miners and their families. The park was the original home of Ferndale RFC between 1882 and 1921.

Rhondda Fach View

Walk Directions: (-) denotes Point of Interest

Leave Aberdare (1) station down the steps and head south across the road towards the Leisure Centre and School. Cross a second road to pick up the path that passes through a gate to the right of the leisure centre building. Follow the path along the river until you come to a footbridge on the right marked Coed Morgannwg Way. Cross the bridge over the river and then cross the road on another footbridge, before passing through a gate onto Violet Street. At end of the street, turn right down Primrose Terrace and then right again down Ynys Lwyd Road to come to a main road opposite the Blaengwawr Inn.

Turn left along this road (Cardiff Road) and then right at the bus stop some 200 meters later, just before the zebra crossing. Pass Blaengwawr Primary School on your right and continue up Gwawr Street and past the newer houses of the Fairways. Turn left up the footpath behind the last of these houses.

The path swings left as it climbs, and you soon come via a gate to

Cross the stile to enter woodland

a crossroads of paths. Turn right along the cycle path and continue along it until you come to a road opposite a waterworks. Turn left along the road and head uphill. Follow the road as it bends right, then take the path that heads off to the left, next to the speed limit sign. Cross the stile and follow the track as it zig-zags uphill to another stile, which you cross to enter a woodland. The path is now less distinct, and in summer can be overgrown with bracken, but it broadly follows the line of the dry stone wall on your left. Make your way uphill, keeping as close to the wall as you can, until you come to another stile leading to a roadside.

Keep to the left of the barrier marking the sharp turn in the road and follow the path that continues uphill, crossing yet another stile to come to an old quarry. The path forks and you should take the right-hand option, climbing a little before passing to the left of the main quarry face. As you approach the fence ahead, bear right to come to another stile (do not be distracted by another track heading downhill to a gate on the left). Cross the stile and follow the track along the hilltop. After about 400 meters you pass under power lines to come to another stile. Here the path forks in three – take the middle path straight ahead through the heather.

The track becomes more distinct and stonier as it drops down the slope towards Cwmaman village, and levels out before making a sharp u-turn. Stay with it, as you head now in a westerly direction with the village to your left. Eventually, you pass through a metal gate to

Take middle path of the three

follow the track past dog kennels and poultry enclosures to come to Brynhyfryd terrace. Turn right and then left to arrive at the main street next to Cwmaman Workmen and Social Club (2). Turn right along the road and then almost immediately left along a track just before the school sign. At the clearing take the path of dark gravel that heads up the embankment in front of you.

The path bears right and climbs through woodland, becoming stonier and steeper. Where it turns sharp left, follow it, ignoring the other less-distinct path that heads off to the right. After a steepish ascent, the path levels out and becomes grassier as it bears right and emerges into a clearing and passes the stone ruins of Bedwlwyn farmstead. Continue uphill through conifers; the climb is more gradual now. Continue straight ahead at a crossroads of paths to emerge some 150 meters later at a forestry track.

Turn left along this track. After about ¾ mile, the forest thins out on the right and disappears completely on the left, giving fine

Boulders at entrance to Roman Camp

views over the Aman and Cynon valleys below. Just before the point where the track is crossed by power cables, a path heads off to the right through boulders to a clearing that marks the site of the Twyn-y-Briddallt Roman Camp (3). Turn right and head across the

138

clearing until you come to the high point at its north-eastern end, where both the views and the remains of the camp defences are at their best. From here, your exit from the camp is found by looking back over the clearing and following the line of the power lines to the point where they enter the woods on the right hand side (the opposite side to that which you entered the site). Head towards that point, but do not follow the power lines into the woods. Rather, you should take the path that passes through another gap in the trees a little to the right. Follow the path as it bears left and then right and emerges onto the open hillside of Craig y Gilwern above the Rhondda Fach. With the valley to your left, continue along the perimeter of the woods for a while before re-entering the forest and descending steeply to join a forestry track.

Turn left along the track and follow it as it descends through the woods. Shortly after passing to the left of two pylons you pass a metal gate and encounter the first houses of Blaenllechau. Continue to descend, now on a metalled road, to a mini roundabout where you continue straight ahead and downhill past Blaenllechau Radical Club and Carmel Chapel. Continue around the sharp bend in the road then over the bridge, and start climbing uphill past the Rugby Club on your right. At the crossroads next to the Anchor Hotel and Trerhondda Independent Chapel (4) cross the zebra crossing across the main street and continue gradually uphill. Turn left at the Conservative Club along Wood Street, and then left at end of the street to come to the gates of Darran Park. Enter the park and follow the path to the lake. Turn right so that the lake is on your left. 100 meters later another path heads off to the right into woodland.

Continue along this path, heading away from the lake, until you pass through a kissing-gate. At the fork, take the left-hand path that climbs gradually. At the next fork take the right-hand path, ignoring the track which climbs more steeply uphill. Pass through a gate and turn right, following the fence until – shortly after passing a ruined dry stone wall – the path bears left uphill and away from the fence. When you are reunited with the fence shortly afterwards, pass through the gap in it that is marked with a black arrow sign on the post. Follow the path as it heads away from the valley and towards the wind turbines on the ridge ahead. Cross a track running alongside another ruined wall to come to a gate in the fence on the crest of the ridge.

Continue straight ahead and downhill so that you pass just to the left of the turbine nearest to you, crossing a gravel track as you do so. Immediately after, you will pick up a clear grassy track heading downhill straight ahead.

Pass through the gate waymarked Loops & Links and continue directly down to another gate similarly marked, and then, having

Pass through waymarked gate

140

crossed a small stream, through a third. Continue downhill, following the fence on your left. As you pass through yet another gate, a clear track emerges. Follow it as it passes to the left of overgrown waste tips. After passing through a metal gate, leave the track through the gate on your right to enter a field, as indicated again by the Loops & Links waymark.

Continue downhill, initially keeping close to the fence on your left before leaving it behind and picking up a path that heads between clumps of gorse to a small metal gate and onwards to a playground. Turn right along the gravel track and continue across stepping stones and around a metal barrier. The path continues to the left of Bryn y Wawr house and passes through a large gate. Keep left at the fork to pass through another, smaller, gate. The path forks again at a disused quarry. At this point, keep to the left to descend quickly through heather and then trees, to emerge at the end of a street next to a bridleway fingerpost. Take the steps down on the left and cross the road to Ton Pentre railway station.

Ton Pentre – Maesteg

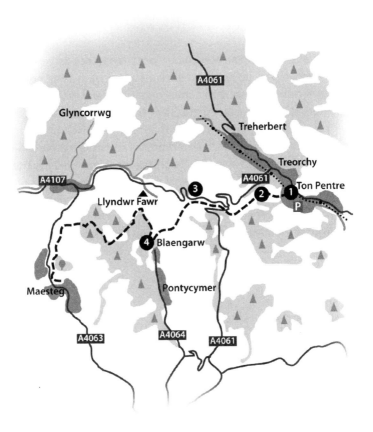

11. Ton Pentre – Maesteg

Approx distance: *13 miles / 21 km*

Approx time: *6.5 hours*

O.S Maps: *1: 50,000 OS Landranger Sheet 171*

1: 25,000 OS Explorer Sheet 166 (recommended)

Start & End: *The walk starts at Ton Pentre railway station and ends at Maesteg station. Both stations have regular trains to Cardiff, which is about an hour away from each. You can also return from Maesteg to Ton Pentre by bus. Plan your journey at www.traveline-cymru.info*

Access: *Ton Pentre is in the Rhondda Fawr just south-east of Treorchy, while Maesteg is 10 miles north of Bridgend on the A4063. Both stations are signposted.*

Parking: *Street parking in Ton Pentre, while Maesteg station has parking.*

Terrain: *Mostly minor paths across open country and hills, with two sections through forestry between Blaengarw and Maesteg, and some brief roadside walking to start and finish.*

Please note: *The walk has a total ascent of 750 meters / 2,475 feet, with most of it coming between Ton Pentre and Bwlch y Clawdd and then from Blaengarw to Llyndwr Fawr, and with plenty of less strenuous walking in between. Much of the walk is across grazed land, so dogs will occasionally need to be on a lead. Some sections can get quite muddy following wet weather.*

Facilities: *There are public toilets near the start point in Ton Pentre, while both Ton Pentre and Maesteg have convenience stores and public houses.*

Points of Interest

1. The Parish Church, Ton Pentre

In pre-Norman times, Glynrhondda was a commote of the Kingdom of Morgannwg, with its 'capital' presumed to have been located in the vicinity of modern-day Maerdy (literally, mayor or steward's house) at the head of the Rhondda Fach. In the late 11th century, the Normans seized control from the last native king of Morgannwg, Iestyn ap Gwrgant, though it would take another two centuries before they had tamed the hills and valleys to the north of the Vale.

Glynrhondda eventually became the parish of Ystradyfodwg, with the parish church – dedicated to the Welsh saint Tyfodwg – located here on the banks of the Rhondda Fawr. B.H. Malkin was not overly impressed with the church when he visited in 1804, finding it to be 'one of the most miserable in its structure, and most neglected in its preservation, of all that have come to my knowledge in travelling through the mountainous parts of south Wales'. He was more impressed with the scenery however, describing the steep imposing hillsides as 'the Alps of Glamorganshire'.

At that time, the Rhondda Fawr was very sparsely populated, and the only place resembling a settlement would have been a cluster of cottages around the fulling mill at Tonypandy. While neighbouring Aberdare and Merthyr were already developing into bustling industrial areas, it would take another half a century before the Rhondda was rudely awoken from its splendid rural isolation, but when it happened it certainly happened with a bang.

The population of Ystradyfodwg in 1801 was a mere 542, and in 1851 it was still only 951. With the sinking of the first deep mines in the 1850s, it multiplied by a factor of twenty-five over a period of twenty years to 23,950 in 1871 and continued to grow

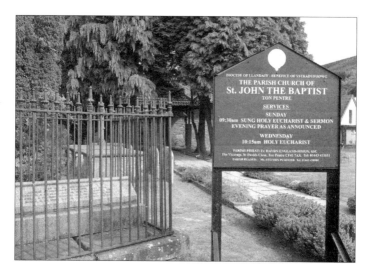

Parish Church – Ton Pentre

expodentially into the twentieth century, reaching an incredible 152,781 by 1911.

The fate of the church has in some ways reflected that of the parish itself. The medieval building was replaced by a new structure in 1893, when it was re-dedicated to St John the Baptist. By that time it had in any case been superceded in size, though not in official status as parish church, by the imposing St Peter's on the opposite bank of the river in Pentre, known as 'the cathedral of the Rhondda'. As the coal industry underwent its final decline, the Victorian church was itself demolished in the 1980s, to be replaced by the modern structure we see today.

2. Maendy Camp

The Maendy Camp fort on Mynydd Maendy is one of the best examples of an Iron Age hillfort in Glamorgan, and is probably the oldest surviving human settlement in the Rhondda. Its location on the end of the Mynydd Maendy ridge means it is surrounded on three sides by steep hillsides, giving it a strong defensive position visible for miles around.

Though much of it is obscured by bracken, the stone rubble reveals the outline of the ancient defences: the inner enclosure being horseshoe-shaped, while the outer defences are more circular. The walls were originally 2.4 metres thick and enclosed an area of over two acres. On the western side, where natural defences are less effective, there were additional ditches and a bank.

Hill forts of this kind started appearing in Britain around 600BC and are particularly common in the south and west, including Wales. The fact that they are commonly situated on prominent hillsides overlooking valuable agricultural land suggests that the forts had some kind of defensive or territorial function. But they may also have had other uses, such as a meeting point for disparate farming communities, market-places, or a communal store for surplus grain over winter. Some may have been permanently inhabited, while others may have been used seasonally or as places of ritual and ceremony.

Excavations at the site in 1901 recovered worked flints, including arrow-heads and knives, and numerous pieces of decorated pottery. A bronze dagger and pieces of an urn were found in an older Bronze Age cairn on the western edge of the camp, showing human activity on Mynydd Maendy as long as 4,000 years ago.

3. Crug yr Afan

The Bronze Age round barrow at Crug yr Afan is the best example of its type in the region, standing on a broad summit that overlooks three vallleys: Cwm Parc to the east, Cwm Ogwr Fawr to the south and the Gwynfi/Afan valley to the west.

In Stone Age Britain communal burials were the norm, but this practice had changed by the Bronze Age, with cremated remains being interred individually in barrows and cairns. The location and size of the Crug yr Afan monument, suggests that it was the final resting place of a person of some import. The barrow itself consists of a mound of clay and stones of around 25 meters in diamater, surrounded by a ditch 2 meters wide. Set on top of the clay mound was a stone cairn, itself 10 meters wide and a meter high and surrounded originally by a ring of standing stones. Excavations in the early 1900s found a cist cut into the earth below the mound containing cremated remains and a bronze dagger.

Both the recovered dagger and the barrow itself are of styles typical of Early Bronze Age Wessex, suggesting close contact and cultural exchange during that period between the peoples of upper Glamorgan and the more established tribes of the lowlands on the other side of the Severn.

Just south of Crug yr Afan, on the other side of the road, are the remains of a bank and ditch of an 8th century cross-dyke. It is one of a number of such embankments found on the hills above the Rhondda (there is another at Bwlch y Clawdd nearby), which served both as boundary markers between the different *cantrefi* (hundreds) of the time, and as check-points on the ancient travel routes along the ridges, to defend the local populace from unwanted or lawless visitors.

4. Blaengarw

More than any other section of the walks in this book, the journey from Ton Pentre to Blaengarw allows an appreciation of the impact of glaciation on the landscape. The heads of Cwm Parc, and the Ogmore (*Ogwr*) and Garw valleys consist of huge amphitheatres carved out by the the glaciers of the last ice age. The melting ice has left behind steep-sided u-shaped valleys,

Cwmparc from Bwlch y Clawdd

Craig Ogwr

Parc Calon Lân – Blaengarw

separated from the moorland plateau by imposing and barely passable sandstone bluffs.

While there are no mountains here in the strict meaning of that term, the terrain is certainly mountainous in its aspect. From the masts on Y Werfa to the river at Blaengarw, the walker loses 400 meters in height in just over a mile. For comparison, the climb from Storey Arms to the top of Pen y Fan is only 50 meters more over a distance twice as long.

Certainly, Blaengarw has the feeling of a frontier about it; no roads breach its surrounding headwalls, and the only way in or out is along the narrow valley floor which stretches southwards in the direction of Bridgend, and beyond it the sea.

Coal mining came to Blaengarw in the late 19th century, with the sinking of the International Colliery on the west bank of the river in 1874, followed by the Ocean (Garw) Colliery to the east in

1886. The former closed in 1968, and the latter in 1985 – one of the wave of closures that sparked the Miners' Strike of that year. The site of the International Colliery, and its associated railway sidings, has now been landscaped to create Parc Calon Lân.

The park is named for the famous Welsh hymn whose words were written by Daniel James (1848 – 1920) while he lived at Herbert Street in the village, and worked underground at the Ocean Colliery. James was known for his love of a drink, and it is said that he earned his beer-money from selling poems. John Hughes, also of Blaengarw, composed the famous tune to accompany James' lyrics, and it was first performed publicly at the Blaengarw Hotel.

Walk Directions: (-) denotes Point of Interest
Turn left out of the train station and then left again over the bridge, passing the church (1) on your right immediately after it. Take the third right (between Spar and Fagin's Bar) down Maindy Road and continue until you come to the Police Station, where you should turn left. Continue uphill, heading out of the village until the road becomes a stony track, signposted 'Loops & Links'.

The track is initially steep and loose before levelling out and becoming grassier. As you emerge onto the Mynydd Maendy ridge, you pass a TV mast on your right, and there is a short marshy section where you pass through a large metal gate. Continue straight ahead, bearing slightly left as you pass the site of Maendy Camp (2) then through a smaller metal gate leading to a gravelly path. Before long another small metal gate leads onto the hillside and past a mysteriously isolated stile. Follow the grassy path uphill, bearing right as you aim for the highest point of the ridge – do not be tempted by another path that bears left. From here you will have stunning views of Cwmparc. Continue along the ridge until you reach Bwlch y Clawdd pass. Go through the small metal gate, cross the road and take the path straight ahead up the embankment.

The path climbs steeply up a slope before levelling out and following the edge of the escarpment of Craig Ogwr, high above the Ogmore (*Ogwr*) valley. The path occasionally forks – you should always take the option that keeps closest to edge of the escarpment on the left, even if it appears to be no more than a sheep track at times. Eventually the path drops down into a marshy area, and you cross a stream then pass through a gate. From the gate, the path is very indistinct for short period; you should continue in the same westerly direction, passing between the clumps of rushes and gaining height very gradually. You may find it useful to aim just to the right of the masts on the horizon ahead. After about 200 meters, the path re-emerges at another stream crossing, and then passes through another marshy area (actually the head of the Ogmore river) before joining a metalled track via a stile.

From here, a short detour from the main route brings you to Crug yr Afan (3). Turn right down the track and then cross the main road, before heading straight uphill on the other side to come to the cairn at the highest point of the flat summit of Twyn Crugyrafan, next to the corner of the forest.

Retrace your steps back to the stile, and continue along the track straight ahead until you come to a cattle grid, where you should take the stony path that heads off to the left. Continue along it until it forks next to a set of metal posts. Here, you should take the grassier path that heads off to the left. Almost immediately, you come to another junction of paths: you should continue straight ahead, passing to the right of a black waymark post. The path is now little more than a sheep's track as it crosses open country in a south-westerly direction, but the black fingerposts appear at regular intervals to show the way until it becomes clearer again as you start zig-zagging downhill towards Blaengarw (4).

Pass through a small metal gate and follow the field perimeter to the right to come to another. Pass through it and head straight downhill to another gate which leads onto a grassy track. Follow this track as it descends towards the village. As it approaches it makes a couple of sharp turns – follow the blue bridleway waymark on each occasion. Another metal gate brings you out onto a narrow road – turn right, then left, then right again to come to the main road. Cross it and continue straight ahead to come to Parc Calon Lân.

Cross the footbridge just upstream of the lake, and then turn right along the path. When the path comes to the road, turn immediately left along a track as indicated by the public footpath

sign. Just before the first hut on the right-hand side of the track, a grassy path heads off uphill as indicated by a bridleway waymark.

Continue along this path until you come to a forestry track. Turn right for a few

Bridleway on right next to hut

meters, until you come to another path on your left, again indicated by a blue bridleway waymark. Follow this path as it continues to climb, keeping left at the fork (bridleway waymark) to come eventually to another forestry track. Turn right along the track, and then left on another path, again as indicated by a bridleway waymark.

The path eventually emerges from the woods, and remains clear – if rather loose – as it climbs steeply to the saddle of Bwlchgarw. A number of paths meet at the saddle, and you should turn left along the path that climbs steeply uphill. The path runs parallel to the edge of the forest – the trig point marking the highest point of the flat summit of Llyndwr Fawr is found a short distance away from the path to your right (north west). Continue to follow the treeline until the path becomes more distinct as it passes through two gates in quick succession.

After the second gate it becomes less clear again, but broadly runs parallel to the fence on your right until the fence changes direction at a right angle, at which point you should carry on through a gap in the rushes to a large metal gate, waymarked Garw Valley Walk, in another fence straight ahead of you. Pass through the gate and continue in the same direction down the middle of the field until, at its far end, you come to a stile at the edge of the woods.

Cross the stile and at the junction of four tracks, take the right-hand one, keeping right again at the fork immediately afterwards. Continue to follow the same track as it descends gradually. After about ¾ mile the track makes a hairpin turn to the right, at which point you should turn off it along the less distinct track on the left. Keep right at the fork soon after, and continue along this track as

Stile to junction of four tracks

it winds it way gradually downhill until you exit the forest at a minor road. Turn right along the road to come to Caerau Primary School.

Turn left along the cycle path – route 885 – that follows the school perimeter fence. Continue to follow this path, which has regular blue signposts, until you arrive in Maesteg at a junction of roads. Turn left down Talbot Terrace / Castle Street and continue until you come to the railway station on your left.

Glossary

aber – river mouth, estuary
afon – river
allt – slope
ar – on. over
bach/fach – little
bedd – grave
blaen – upland, limit, source
bre – hill
brith – speckled, mottled
bryn – hill
bugail – shepherd
bwlch – pass
caer(au) – fort(s)
canol – middle, centre
capel – chapel
carn/garn – cairn
carreg, pl. *cerrig* – rock, stone
castell – castle
cefn – ridge
cil – nook, source of stream
cilfach – nook, retreat
clawdd – dyke
coch – red
coed – wood
*cors/gor*s – bog, marsh
craig – rock, cliff
crib – ridge
croes – cross
crug – cairn

cwm – valley
dan – under
dau – two
deri – oak trees
dinas – hill fort
dôl – meadow
du/ddu – black
dŵr – water
efail – smithy/forge
eglwys – church
fan – hill
ffordd – road
ffrwd – stream, torrent
ffynnon – well
gelli – grove
glan – river bank
glas – blue, green
glyn – valley
gwaith – works
gwaun/waun – moor, heath
gwyn/gwen – white
gwynt – wind
hafod – summer dwelling
hen – old
hendre – winter dwelling
heol – road
isaf – lower
llan pl. *llannau* – church, village
llyn – lake

llwybr – path, track
llwyn – grove, bush
maen – rock, stone
maes – field
marchog – knight
mawr/fawr – great, big
melin – mill
melyn – yellow
moel/foel – bare topped hill
mynydd – mountain, hill
nant – brook, stream
newydd – new
ogof – cave
parc – field, park
pen – head, top
pentre – village
plas – hall
pont – bridge
porth – gateway
pridd – earth, soil
pwll – pool
rhiw – hill, slope
rhyd – ford
sant – saint
tafarn – inn
tarren/darren – steep hill, scarp
teg – fair
tir – land
ton – meadow
traeth – beach
tre(f) – town, hamlet
troed – foot

twyn – hill
tŷ – house
uchaf – upper
wiwer – squirrel
y/yr – the
yn – in
ynys – island, river meadow
ysgol – school

A series of guide books to take you to every corner
of this magnificent walking country

- Short family walks
- Excellent coastal
  walks
- Hill and mountain
  walks & panoramic
  views
- Level lakeside and
  valley walks
- Woodland and
  nature walks
- Fascinating heritage
  and history guides
- Clear coloured maps
- Route photos and
  attractions on the way
- Updated directions

www.carreg-gwalch.com

SNOWDONIA

160 pages of Carreg Gwalch

BEST LAKESIDE WALKS

- Coloured maps
- Route photos
- Updated directions
- Heritage notes

SNOWDONIA

160 pages of Carreg Gwalch

BEST WOODLAND WALKS

- Coloured maps
- Route photos
- Updated directions
- Heritage notes

SNOWDONIA

160 pages of Carreg Gwalch

BEST VALLEY WALKS

- Coloured maps
- Route photos
- Updated directions
- Heritage notes

160 pages of Carreg Gwalch

ANGLESEY

BEST WALKS

160 pages of Carreg Gwalch

LLŶN

BEST WALKS

- Coloured maps
- Route photos
- Updated directions
- Heritage notes

160 pages of Carreg Gwalch

CONWY VALLEY

BEST WA

BEST WALKS

- Coloured maps
- Route photos
- Updated directions
- Heritage notes

- Coloured maps
- Route photos
- Updated directions
- Heritage notes